THIS IS FASCISM

A WAKE-UP CALL

Rosan Smits

Atlantic Books
London

First published in the Netherlands as *Dit is fascisme* in 2025 by
De Correspondent.

First published in paperback in Great Britain in 2026 by Atlantic Books,
an imprint of Atlantic Books Ltd.

10 9 8 7 6 5 4 3 2

A CIP catalogue record for this book is available from the British Library.

Paperback ISBN: 978 1 80546 656 7
E-book ISBN: 978 1 80546 657 4

Printed and bound by CPI (UK) Ltd, Croydon CR0 4YY

Atlantic Books
An imprint of Atlantic Books Ltd
Ormond House
26–27 Boswell Street
London
WC1N 3JZ

www.atlantic-books.co.uk

Product safety EU representative: Authorised Rep Compliance Ltd., Ground Floor,
71 Lower Baggot Street, Dublin, D02 P593, Ireland. www.arccompliance.com

THIS IS FASCISM

'This book is a distress signal. Rosan Smits makes it crystal clear how fascism is being normalized at alarming speed. Think it can't happen in Western democracies? Then read this book – because it already is' Rutger Bregman, bestselling author of *Moral Ambition*

'An excellent read' Timothy Snyder, bestselling author of *On Tyranny*

'After a decade of debate about the nature of the global far right, Rosan Smits amasses the evidence and the competing analyses to produce a definitive judgment: this is fascism. A necessary read to understand the challenge we face now from the xenophobic ideology destroying democracies across the west' Jason Stanley, bestselling author of *How Fascism Works*

'A masterful and chilling dissection of the modern ideology of hate' Paul Mason, author of *How to Stop Fascism*

'Few journalists address the major issues of our time. Rosan Smits does. She explains clearly and convincingly what fascism is and why we need to use the word now. A necessary book' Simon Kuper, bestselling author of *Chums*

'This book is a mirror. And we would be foolish not to look' Carice van Houten

Rosan Smits is a political scientist who has conducted research on radicalization and violence in war zones for many years. She led the Conflict Research Unit at the Netherlands Institute of International Relations. Since 2017, she has been deputy editor-in-chief of *De Correspondent*.

Contents

Introduction   1

Part 1: This is fascism

1. The fascist playbook   13

Part 2: Today's fascism

2. Fascism has a new face: the Trump regime   37

3. Fascist patterns in Europe today   58

4. A case study: the fascist playbook in the
    Netherlands   87

Part 3: Building a dam against fascism

5. Together against fascism   111

6. The foundations: politics that fight back   117

7. The protective layer: resilient journalism   126

8. The barrier: society in solidarity   135

Acknowledgements   143

Notes   145

Introduction

Early in February 2025, a video appeared on X. A US immigration officer can be seen patting down someone before deportation. In the background, Seattle airport, a plane readying for departure, its engines idling.

Then, the rattle of metal: a blue plastic crate filled with cuffs on chains. Someone is laying them out in lines on the tarmac – one set per person. People are being cuffed tightly, hands and feet. The camera shows no faces, only bodies and irons. The video ends with a shackled detainee struggling up the steel aircraft stairs, their chains clanking against the metal steps.

The title of the post: 'ASMR: Illegal Alien Deportation Flight 🔊'. That abbreviation is a wry reference to the genre of online videos intended to induce a safe, soothing feeling through certain sounds – think of whispers, the rhythmic tapping of raindrops or the rustling of leaves in the wind. In this case, the sounds of heavily chained people being deported.

The source of the post: the White House.[1]

Alarm bells are ringing

Fascism is back. This time not with swastikas, Nazi flags and deadly bureaucracy, but Make America Great Again caps, right-wing extremist memes and a fist raised in triumph. Not ghettos and concentration camps, but data-driven manhunts and 'detention facilities' in El Salvador and Guantánamo Bay. Not brownshirts and SS squads, but masked immigration officers and a Capitol-storming mob.

It's crystal clear: in his second term as president of the United States, Donald Trump is putting together a fascist regime. And fast. Not only Trump's political adversaries say so;[2] his own former advisers do too.[3] What's more, internationally renowned scholars – experts in the field of fascism – are sounding the alarm. A number of them have exited the United States entirely, sending out a powerful message: *Take it from us, fascism is here.*[4] In 2025, over 400 scholars from more than thirty countries signed an open letter against fascism. The evidence is overwhelming, they said: fascism is on the rise. Not just in the US, but around the world.[5]

Resistance to the warning

Such warnings about fascism have met with resistance. Some believe that the label of 'fascist' quells any debate before it can start; that it's become a slur for anyone people disagree with, flung around so freely it has lost its meaning.

Some take this to another extreme: anyone who accuses them of being fascist gets called 'fascist' right back.[6] It is a tried-and-true tactic to strip language of its meaning: if everyone labels their adversaries 'fascist', the word loses its power to warn people about *actual* fascism. Even when the term is apt, the debate invariably derails into a squabble over the word itself, wholesale ignoring what warranted its use.

This can be a reason to opt instead for the more general term 'authoritarianism', which covers a range of political systems and movements that concentrate power around a 'strongman' – including fascism.[7] But this would leave us unable to call out why millions are again voting for authoritarian leadership: they back an extremist agenda based on a strongman's promise of national rebirth and a belief that their own cultural group is superior. Fascism.

For others, the label of 'fascism' is inextricably linked to the revolutionary spirit of the interwar period. In their eyes, that twentieth-century brand of fascism simply does not map onto today's politics. Worse, they warn, forcing the comparison could blind us to what is genuinely new about the threats democracy now faces.

History doesn't repeat itself; it echoes into the present. Today's fascism differs from that of the past; it is closely intertwined with post-war populism and less explosive than Benito Mussolini ever envisioned.[8] But make no mistake: leaders of today are working from templates drawn up back then. Making this connection between past and present is a prerequisite for understanding what democracy is up against – and for defending its existence.

But by far the greatest resistance to the use of the term 'fascism' comes from people who simply see it as exaggerated and alarmist, because today's far-right populists pale in comparison to Adolf Hitler. Calling them 'fascists', they believe, is like shouting 'Fire!' when someone lights a candle. The reasoning goes like this: *If we call this fascism, what word do we use when it gets worse?* Or, conversely: *It's only when you no longer dare call a regime fascist that it is fascist.*[9]

Granted, as long as you can openly oppose fascism, you are not living under a fascist regime – yet. But fascist movements take root long before that threshold. They start with violent language: talk of 'invasions' and 'national suicide', calls to 'fight back', and the creeping normalization of dehumanizing, excluding or expelling entire groups. All in the name of national security.

Fascism thrives on the normalization of ideas that were once considered extremist. And it is precisely the idea that 'it cannot happen here' that is so conducive to its rise. This presents scholars with an almost unsolvable dilemma: warn early, and you are dismissed as an alarmist. But once the threat is undeniable, it's too late.

Radicalization, repression, violence

Despite this, many experts are now raising the alarm. They recognize a pattern: societies start to break up due to mistrust; radicalization follows, then repression, then violence. In a democratic society, this can be fascism's point of entry.

I know that pattern too. I have seen it up close: in war zones, in authoritarian states, across years of work as a political scientist for aid organizations, think tanks, and multilateral institutions like the United Nations.

In 2003, I saw it in Iran, where a peaceful student protest was met with brutal state violence and a wave of arrests – a pattern that has played out in that country regularly ever since.

I saw it two years later in Israel and occupied Palestine, during the tense time after the Second Intifada. Israel had already begun building its illegal separation wall in the West Bank and would soon seal off the Gaza Strip entirely.[10] A significant step in a long escalation towards the genocide of the Palestinian people that Israel is currently committing.

Between 2006 and 2010, I saw it in Sudan, where the Arab regime in Khartoum treated the African population as second-class citizens. After a brutal civil war, South Sudan eventually broke away in 2011. In Darfur, in western Sudan, persecution grew into a genocide. That violence reignited in the region in 2023, displacing more than 14 million people[11] and pushing some 25 million into acute famine.[12]

Between 2007 and 2011, I saw it in Rwanda, where genocide had claimed more than a million lives over a decade earlier. In the years that followed, the violence had spread across the region. In Burundi and the Democratic Republic of Congo, the conflict culminated in the deadliest war since 1939–45.[13]

Again and again, I have seen societies reach the point where propaganda, scapegoating and radicalization make brutal violence seem inevitable. And it's people like you and me who become the victims of that violence.

In the US and Europe too

In 2016, a similar pattern emerged here in the West: politicians were talking about 'our people first' again.

Donald Trump was elected president of the United States for the first time. He not only promised to build a 'big and beautiful' border wall to stop the 'invasion' of immigrants, but also to go after his political opponent, Hillary Clinton – 'Lock her up! Lock her up!'[14]

That same year, British citizens voted to leave the European Union. The Brexit campaign capitalized on societal discontent and nationalist sentiment with a torrent of disinformation. Mistrust, lies and a common enemy: the slow killers of democracy.

All this unfolded as millions of Syrians, Iraqis, Afghans and others were fleeing to Europe.[15] In Germany, Chancellor Angela Merkel's resolute *wir schaffen das* attitude was overtaken by right-wing conspiracy theories about a 'Great Replacement' and the 'dilution of the Western peoples'.

This resulted in the EU's toughened asylum and border policy, in which deterrence and dehumanization became more important than human rights or compassion. The image of Aylan Kurdi – the Syrian toddler whose lifeless body washed ashore on a Turkish beach in 2015 – shocked the world. But it changed nothing. The fences around Fortress Europe only got higher, the coast guards more aggressive, and the migration deals with dictators more shameless.

It was these events that made me change careers from being a conflict researcher to deputy editor-in-chief of the journalistic platform *De Correspondent* – because when politics fails, journalism can still hold the line.

For the past decade, the West has been in a state of constant unrest. Inverted flags, burning hay bales, and tractors on the motorways. Climate activists and yellow vests blocking the roads. #MeToo. Black Lives Matter. Covid-19 lockdowns and curfews, and anti-vaxxers taking to the streets. War on the European continent. Israel's genocide of the Palestinians. Rearmament. Trump *again*.

In my own country, the Netherlands, everything has been dubbed a crisis: the climate crisis, the refugee crisis, the nitrogen crisis, the energy crisis, the cost-of-living crisis, the housing crisis. One government crisis is followed by the next, then another and another.

Meanwhile, elsewhere in the world, heatwaves, wildfires and floods have broken one record after another. And we have stayed glued to our screens, doomscrolling through the ominous headlines, fed by algorithms that only amplify the polarization and scapegoating.

Scapegoating is the political currency of the far-right politicians who have gained ground everywhere in recent years. I've seen their kind of politics before. But the way it unfolds in established democracies is different from what happens in countries like Sudan or the Democratic Republic of Congo. It works through elections and coalitions, through weaponizing language and wielding the law – gradually undermining democracy from within. This phenomenon has a name: fascism.

Naming it helps us grasp it. And shows us what we can *do* about it.

Naming, understanding and combating fascism

For most people, the term 'fascism' immediately evokes historical images of Adolf Hitler's Third Reich or Benito Mussolini's Blackshirts. Some might think of Francisco Franco's generals or perhaps the white pointed hoods of the Ku Klux Klan. The word carries strong connotations – ones that don't immediately square with the politics of

Donald Trump, Viktor Orbán or Geert Wilders. But appearances can be deceiving. The key markers of fascism are not swastika banners or dictators with little moustaches.

So how *can* we recognize it? There's no one-size-fits-all definition of fascism, but there are a few rules of thumb.

One: not every fascist is an autocrat, and not every autocrat is a fascist. Fascism can manifest as ideas and convictions, as social movements supporting an authoritarian leader, and in some rare cases it can ultimately result in a fascist dictatorship. Absolute rule – or autocracy – is a form of government without citizen participation or institutional checks on power. It might be a military dictatorship like Myanmar, a one-party state like North Korea, an absolute monarchy like Saudi Arabia or a fascist state like Nazi Germany. Autocrats come in all ideological colours. They're not necessarily violent, though history offers no shortage of evidence to the contrary. Take Joseph Stalin: under the guise of communism's radical equality, he had an estimated 6 million people murdered[16] – one of the most horrendous crimes against humanity, but not a case of fascism.[17]

Two: all Nazis were fascists, but not all fascists are Nazis. Fascism revolves around the notions that one's own cultural group is superior, and that the nation is in decline due to a conspiracy of minorities and left-wing liberal elites. Those core ideas keep returning – in different forms, depending on the time, the place and the crises of the day. In the early 1990s, historian Roger Griffin therefore defined fascism as 'a genus of political ideology whose mythic core in its various permutations is a palingenetic form of populist ultranationalism'.[18] Or, to put it more simply, a belief in national rebirth through the victory of one's own people, by purging outsiders and ousting a 'corrupt' elite. At the same time, Griffin warned against using ideology as the prime marker to recognize fascism's contemporary variants. Fascism only really becomes visible in *practice*, he said: in the ways those ideas are translated into texts, propaganda, policy, organizations, institutions and concrete actions.[19]

Three: fascism may change its forms, but never its methods. You can therefore identify today's fascism by paying attention to what political leaders and their voters do and say. It is helpful here to consider another influential approach, this time formulated by the American historian Robert Paxton, emeritus professor of history and political science at Columbia University and author of *The Anatomy of Fascism* (2004). Looking at many fascist movements side by side, he noticed they all shared something beyond ideology: a way of operating.

Think of it as a strategy, by which a shaky pact of far-right and ultra-conservative politicians and business elites seizes power by responding to societal discontent, 'marked by obsessive preoccupation with community decline, humiliation or victimhood'.[20] Unlike definitions that focus on fascism primarily as an ideology, Paxton emphasizes the *function* fascism serves for far-right politicians and their followers within a democracy.

Paxton's work has greatly influenced recent standard works on democratic backsliding. His definition removes fascism from its historical context and identifies its behavioural patterns, providing a useful framework for recognizing fascism in its contemporary forms.

That is why his approach serves as my starting point. The first part of this book will show how the fascist playbook works and how its methods can be recognized today. This is essential knowledge for anyone who cherishes their freedom. Because if fascism is recognized in time, democracy can be protected against it.

In the second part, I will describe the rise of contemporary fascism: how it has transformed the United States, why that's not just an American but also a European problem, and what the situation is here in the Netherlands. But fascism is back worldwide, scholars say, not just in the US and Europe. So why focus on these two continents? This book is an attempt to break away from the strongly held conviction in the West that our established democracies are immune to the threat of fascism. They are not. The West isn't just where fascism was born, it is where its new variants are being incubated. And these modern variants not only pose a threat to our national democracies, but also to the international rules-based order built on law and human rights. The illusion that Western democracies are now better shielded from this danger than they were a hundred years ago makes us vulnerable and apathetic, precisely at a moment when action is still possible.

Standing up against emerging fascism requires collective action; nothing is inevitable in politics. The best response, as I'll explain in the final part of this book, is to beat fascism at its own game: mass mobilization. Fascism doesn't stand a chance if enough people understand that an attack on one person's freedom is an attack on *everyone's* freedom.

If, in short, enough people understand: this is fascism.

PART 1

This is fascism

It happened once and it can happen again.
This is the heart of what we have to say.

— Primo Levi, Jewish Italian writer and chemist, *The Drowned and the Saved* (1987), translated by Michael F. Moore

1. The fascist playbook

You can recognize fascism by the way certain politicians capitalize on societal discontent to mobilize a dominant cultural group against an alleged enemy. It is a method of coming into power through democratic means and then retaining that power by dispensing with those means – always in the name of 'the will of the people'.

See it as a playbook. It unfolds step by step, and the components are always the same: a yearning for some idealized, mythical past; a profound contempt for facts; and the accusation that leftist elites and minorities are conspiring to destroy the country – as well as the dominant, often-white majority. In order to restore the nation to its supposed former glory, fascism promises to break radically with the established order and purge society of all 'undesirable influences'. This appeals to voters who have lost faith in traditional politics and institutions.

Steeped in racism and ultranationalism, fascism is rooted in the Social Darwinist idea of survival of the fittest. As Martinican author and politician Aimé Césaire argued, this is colonialism coming home to roost, if in a new form. In his influential essay 'Discourse on Colonialism' (1950), Césaire showed how the brutal racism and extreme violence that European powers normalized in their colonies created the conditions for fascism to emerge back in Europe. Ideas about white superiority, and the repression of people considered to be inferior, returned to the European continent as soon as they served a function for politicians within the democratic context. Fascism was colonialism's inevitable blowback: the racism, dehumanization and extreme violence that had been unleashed on those under colonial rule would also poison European politics itself.[1]

In the fascist worldview, democracy simply means the will of 'the people', embodied by the will of a political strongman. This is contrary to liberal democracy, which aims to *check* the power of leaders and protect minorities from the tyranny of the majority. 'Fascism rejects in democracy the absurd conventional lie of political equalitarianism,' Mussolini wrote in 1932. Instead, fascism could be defined as an 'organized, centralized, authoritarian democracy'.[2]

Fascism lacks a comprehensive, unambiguous ideological narrative. 'Fascist ideology is not a closed body of thought but rather the glorification of very basic and destructive ideas,' writes historian and fascism expert Federico Finchelstein, referring to ideas around xenophobia, violence, authoritarianism and propaganda.[3] Where communism is based on Karl Marx's *Das Kapital* and liberalism is rooted in the thinking of philosophers such as Alexis de Tocqueville and John Stuart Mill, fascism filches its ideas from anywhere. The result, writes the Italian semiotician and author Umberto Eco, is 'a beehive of contradictions'.[4]

This doesn't mean that fascist movements have no main goal; they all strive for a future in which one strong, pure homogeneous community is in power – in the nation and possibly beyond. But to justify that ideal, they nab concepts from existing political or philosophical systems, often in a simplified form – making fascism, at its core, about an absolute conviction in a set of basic, destructive ideas. One that may, but need not, evolve into a fully developed ideology, such as the Nazis demonstrated.

Fascism is, furthermore, fuelled by emotions: anger, resentment, and a hatred of people seen as the enemy. 'A fascist just has to be a storyteller,' historian Timothy Snyder says. 'The stories don't need to be consistent. They don't need to accord with external reality.' A fascist only has to 'find a pulse and hold it'.[5] Fascist movements are therefore difficult to capture in one single definition. As fascism derives its strength from ultranationalist ideas about 'one's own group', each country and each era gets its own version – Adolf Hitler's Nazism, for instance, was different from Mussolini's fascism.

Later, variants such as neofascism[6] appeared, and contemporary movements with fascist characteristics have been described variously as schizofascism,[7] hedofascism,[8] cloud fascism,[9] end-times fascism[10] and wannabe fascism.[11] All these definitions help us better understand the specific characteristics of fascism within their own context – because of course there are differences between then and now or there and here. Understanding these differences is key to understanding specific movements, but it is just as necessary to see what connects them: a shared strategy, a playbook.

Fascism, Mussolini said, 'was born of the need for action, and was action'.[12] Or, as historian Robert Paxton writes in his seminal work *The Anatomy of Fascism*, 'what fascists did tells us at least as much as what they said'.[13]

In other words: you'll know a fascist by what they do.

Right-wing: populism or fascism?

What fascists are doing now, however, looks a lot like post-war radical right-wing populism. Like fascist leaders, radical-right populists promise that their strong leader will fight 'corrupt elites' and put their 'own people' above all else. That is why some scholars call radical right-wing populism 'fascism light'[14] or 'fascism in a democratic key'.[15]

For a long time, radical right-wing populism was not seen as a threat to democracy. The extreme-right, fascist danger seemed safely buried under the rubble of World War II; post-war right-wing populists respected the limits of democracy. 'In the late 1990s, political scientists even considered the rise of right-wing populism healthy for democracy,' Sarah de Lange, professor of Dutch politics at the Institute of Political Science at Leiden University, told me, 'because it meant previously unheard groups got political representation.' Right-wing populism was seen as a call for a different, more direct form of democracy, certainly not as a threat to the system itself. Now, that view is shifting, according to de Lange: 'What we're seeing is that these right-wing populist parties are radicalizing, and the dividing line between the radical and the extreme right has become wafer-thin.'

Because of that wafer-thin line, political scientists nowadays prefer to speak of the 'far right' as an umbrella term for both the radical and the extreme right. We should no longer think of them as two distinct categories, but as part of a spectrum. At one end of that spectrum, there's the radical right – which formally remains within the limits of democracy, but is still chipping away at keystones such as the judiciary and the constitution. At the other end, there's the extreme right, where an authoritarian leader seizes more and more power, and democracy is hollowed out to a facade.

The next step in understanding far-right populism requires us to stop seeing it as a separate political category existing *alongside* fascism (a 'light' version). They are two interconnected movements that are merging into a contemporary fascism built on racism, propaganda, political violence and, ultimately, the undermining of democracy.

Consider this: a far-right populist politician who participates in elections will at first play by the rules and therefore behave as though they were on the radical right. They put pressure on democracy, though as yet not with the intention of destroying it. But their strategy of mobilizing fear and hatred can trigger a radicalization of their politics that leads to the rejection of democratic norms and institutions – pushing them to the extreme right. This is now happening worldwide, as Federico Finchelstein writes in his book *The Wannabe Fascists* (2024): 'Global populism is turning into fascism, and this trend represents a major threat to the future of democracy.'

More on that later. First: the framework by which we can recognize today's fascism.

The five stages of fascism

In *The Anatomy of Fascism*, Robert Paxton shows how fascism unfolds step by step – from the voicing of societal discontent to far-right populism all the way to explicit fascism, when the political rules of the game are abandoned and an authoritarian regime takes hold.

Paxton distinguishes five stages in the fascist strategy:

1. **Creating fascist movements:** Crisis perception and discontent often create a breeding ground for the core ideas of fascism.

2. **Taking root:** A political party forms around a leader.

3. **Seizing power:** The party gains access to political power through democratic elections.

4. **Exercising power:** Political power grows into state power; the movement works to erode fundamental rights and eliminate any institutions meant to check this power. This leads to open fascism.

5. **Radicalization or entropy:** The fascist regime radicalizes further – or loses direction and crumbles.

Although each phase builds on the previous one, a fascist movement need not go through all the phases or develop in only one direction. Many movements get stuck in one stage, fall back, or straddle several stages simultaneously. Still, this framework can help us to understand how contemporary fascism works – rooted as it is in what we know as post-war far-right populism.

Stages 1 and 2: Origin and organization

It starts with the emergence of a movement. The breeding ground for fascism – social discontent, racism, a susceptibility to authoritarianism[16] – is latently present in all democracies. It gains traction when politicians exploit this, typically when a society is under pressure from a crisis, such as a war, a pandemic, an economic recession, or a political impasse. 'Fascism exists at the level of Stage One within all democratic countries,' Paxton writes. In the second half of the twentieth century, this manifested as far-right populism; today, such movements increasingly exhibit openly fascist traits. 'Democracy erodes from the top,' political science professor Larry Bartels concludes in his book of the same name.[17] He envisions an ever-present far-right reservoir which politicians can tap into long as the conditions are right. In the first two stages of fascism, these politicians need not pose a threat, says Paxton: 'As long as they remain excluded from the alliances with the establishment necessary to join the political mainstream or share power… they remain more a law and order problem than a political threat.'

Stage 3: Seizing power

Paxton warns that these movements can gain power rapidly – the third stage – when established conservative and right-wing elites adopt their ideas, talking points and behaviour in order to retain their voters.[18]

In other words: by ignoring developments that set off alarm bells – such as contempt for judges, hostility towards journalists and the stoking of hatred against minorities – and treating far-right politicians who draw on the fascist playbook as 'ordinary' political players, established elites can inadvertently help bring nascent fascist movements to power.

Traditional right-wing and conservative politicians are often willing to cooperate with emerging fascist parties because they share political interests. They want stricter migration policies, for example, or to curtail a woman's right to choose – issues that fascist movements appropriate, exploit, and then turn into existential threats against their 'own people'. Above all, those on the right wing cooperate because they dislike left-wing parties even more.

What's also important is that fascist leaders initially gain their power through elections with the support of voters dissatisfied with established right-wing parties. Traditional right-wing politicians then justify their cooperation with the new party by saying that 'the people have spoken' – a claim that is difficult for any proponent of democracy to dispute.

It's a persistent misconception that such cooperation will moderate fascist movements and bring voters back to their traditional base. A study of the far right's government participation or support in fifty-seven countries by Heike Klüver at Berlin's Humboldt University showed the opposite: 'Government inclusion does not break the appeal of the far right, it consolidates their electoral position.'[19]

The corporate world and the media play a similar role in normalizing far-right views, as the idea that 'the people have spoken' usually shapes how the media approach leaders employing fascist strategies after they win an election. Journalists and talk show hosts help normalize these leaders by giving them a platform as though they were ordinary politicians. Research by British political scientists shows that even when journalists question these politicians critically, the attention still leads the public to develop a greater affinity for extremist views, and to assume that these ideas are widely shared in society. In short: that they are *normal*.[20]

Stage 4: Exercise of power

In the first three stages, fascism can be difficult to recognize, because it's still generally operating within the confines of democracy. But treating these leaders as ordinary politicians is a catastrophic miscalculation. It is exactly how forces that undermine democracy are normalized, Paxton argues. The logical consequence is that more voters will cast their ballots for these fascist leaders, allowing them to exercise real power. And fascists are using democracy to play their own game – one that doesn't end with their term in office, but by seizing absolute power.

Again and again, history has shown how the normalization of extremism unfolds: conservative and right-wing politicians are made complicit or dependent on a fascist movement, then are voted out or actively excluded from the next elections. The left-wing opposition is done away with next, and the separation of powers that holds up liberal democracy implodes once and for all. With this, the fascist regime has taken hold.

That anti-democrats can be democratically elected is an inherent feature of democracy. As early as 360

BCE, Plato warned: 'And so tyranny naturally arises out of democracy.'[21] According to him, the people would eventually turn against the ruling elite and rally behind a tyrant who promised to drive that elite out. More than twenty-three centuries later, in 1928, Joseph Goebbels reiterated the same idea – only to cynically exploit it himself. 'The big joke on democracy is that it hands its mortal enemies the means of its own destruction,' the future Nazi propaganda minister wrote.[22]

Stage 5: Radicalization or entropy

Democracy is threatened by its enemies. Fascism is ultimately destroyed by itself. In this final stage, the regime becomes unstable and self-destructive, Paxton explains, resting as it does on a shaky pact between the democratically elected authoritarian leader, right-wing conservative politicians and ideologues who support this leader, and other power brokers such as religious institutions, media magnates and industrialists.

Paxton believes that this is why, instead of calling fascism an autocracy, it is better to speak of a 'polycracy': a system in which multiple powers coexist, cooperate and compete. Historically, he writes, 'fascist regimes could not settle down into a comfortable enjoyment of power. The charismatic leader had made dramatic promises.' Thus the leader has to keep saving 'their people' from 'the enemy'.

Fail to do so and a fascist movement disintegrates, transforming into an inert authoritarian regime that barely holds itself together. When the leader is no longer 'saving the nation', there's no compelling narrative to sustain their power. The regime then faces a choice: suppress any competitors with violence and fear, as in a military dictatorship, or keep up the appearance that the leader still has a popular mandate.

Increasingly, what happens in this fifth stage is the latter: far-right leaders use fascist methods to undermine democracy but never establish a full-fledged dictatorship.[23] A marginal space for opposition is left intact, but democratic institutions are put to the personal use of the regime, which thus stays in the saddle. This has recently been defined as 'competitive authoritarianism' or 'electoral autocracy' – to describe Hungary, for example.[24]

But if a fascist leader sticks to the narrative of fighting the 'enemy' and continues down the path of mass mobilization, Paxton teaches us, they enter the most extreme phase of the fascist ascent: radicalization. Facing an 'ever-mounting spiral of ever more daring challenges', fanaticism is given free rein. Or, as Umberto Eco put it, in fascism, 'there is no struggle for life but, rather, life is lived for struggle... This, however, brings about an Armageddon complex. Since enemies have to be defeated, there must be a final battle, after which the movement will have control of the world.'[25] At this point, fascist regimes become extremely violent and even genocidal, at home *and* abroad. This is what many people think of when they hear the term 'fascism'.

Such radicalization cannot be sustained in the long term. The climax of unrestrained fascism, therefore, is not world domination, but self-destruction – a society in ruins. There is only one twentieth-century example of this form of radicalization: Adolf Hitler's Third Reich.

Ten instruments to mobilize 'the people'

The fascist strategy unfolds gradually. It thrives on normalizing what was previously considered extremist. Then any warning can be dismissed as alarmist. So how can experts identify the rise of fascism as it is happening? How do we recognize it in time?

Countless checklists claiming to do just that are circulating. You can find them in sleek infographics online, on T-shirts and sweatshirts, and on large placards or on stickers on lamp posts. These warnings are almost always printed in red, black and white – the harsh colours of the Nazi flag – and often using 1930s-style fonts. Some of these lists seem to be cobbled together from such wildly divergent definitions, strategies and exploits associated with fascism, they're close to becoming just as much of a jumble as fascism itself.

To recognize fascism, it helps to distinguish between political behaviour and the ways that behaviour is justified. To expose fascist patterns, we should pay attention to not just what leaders do, but also what they say – their rhetoric. In this context, Paxton speaks of 'mobilizing passions':[26] the emotional mobilization of the masses through which nascent fascism acquires power and ultimately radicalizes. In other words: the fuel that powers fascism from its earliest stirrings to its most extreme stage.

The American political philosopher Jason Stanley builds on this in his book *How Fascism Works* (2018). He distinguishes ten instruments of such mobilization, which are interpreted here with some freedom.[27] Individually, these instruments are used by other political movements, Stanley says, but fascism always uses all ten. This is part of the fascist playbook, which leaders worldwide are adapting and tailoring to today's discontent, wittingly or not – but we'll get to that.

Mythic past

Every fascist invokes a mythic past to justify their tales of a glorious future. If emotion is fascism's fuel, then a people's mythic past is the well from which the fascist draws, stirring up feelings of anger, victimhood and pride.

Adolf Hitler dreamed of a Third Reich in the tradition of the first German empire that lasted a thousand years, and Benito Mussolini promised twentieth-century Italians a return to the splendour of the Roman empire. 'We have created our myth. The myth is a faith, a passion,' Mussolini declared in a 1922 speech. 'And to this myth, this greatness, which we want to translate into a total reality, we subordinate everything.'[28]

Propaganda

Every fascist uses propaganda to stir up feelings of mistrust and disrupt public debate. If the mythic past is the well and emotion, the fuel, propaganda is the machine fascists use to mobilize the masses. As Adolf Hitler said in *Mein Kampf*: 'The art of propaganda lies in understanding the emotional ideas of the great masses.'[29]

The aim is to unite the 'pure nation' by identifying and eliminating those supposedly responsible for its decline: domestic and foreign 'enemies' held accountable for tearing it apart. A fascist will always single out groups that are already relatively vulnerable: Jewish people, the

Roma and Sinti, LGBTQI+ people, migrants, et cetera. A fascist is like a schoolyard bully who terrorizes others in order to improve their own position.

In order for the propaganda to stick, a fascist needs to repeat it over and over again. As Hitler argued: 'All effective propaganda must be limited to a very few points and must harp on these in slogans until the last member of the public understands what you want him to understand by your slogan.'[30]

Anti-intellectualism

Every fascist deliberately undermines any independent thinker who argues with their propaganda. Because people like journalists, artists and academics use their critical thinking to throw sand in the gears of the propaganda machine.

A fascist will portray them as part of a conspiracy, citing as evidence that these opponents discount or contradict the fascists' own conspiracy theories. They denounce journalists and academics as untrustworthy – unless those journalists and academics are sympathetic to their cause – and instead use their own platforms and conduits to spread their propaganda. As soon as possible, a fascist will curtail the media's independence and 'purge' educational and cultural institutions.

In order to systematically suppress critical thinking in society, every fascist ultimately seizes control of the meaning of language itself. They will, for example, invoke freedom of expression to silence critics and label those seeking to safeguard democracy as 'anti-democratic'.

Umberto Eco emphasizes that every fascist uses simple language reminiscent of Orwellian Newspeak, 'an impoverished vocabulary, and an elementary syntax, in order to limit the instruments for complex and critical reasoning'.[31] This form of language almost seems designed for the messages on social media platforms like X – which in turn become the megaphone of contemporary fascism.

Unreality

Every fascist destroys the truth. By undermining public debate and censoring criticism, the propaganda machine is given free rein to strip facts of their authority, rob society of the ability to think independently, and create an alternative reality.

Every fascist does this by lying brazenly and frequently – not to convince people of the lie, but of the idea that there is no truth but the one he decrees. Russian-American journalist M. Gessen calls this the 'bully lie' or the 'power lie'. Such lies serve multiple purposes at once: mobilization, loyalty and domination.[32] They reinforce supporters' deeply held beliefs and grievances and also function as a loyalty test, because they force people to choose between the facts and the fascist's demonstrably false alternative truths. When facts lose all meaning, there's also no need to be consistent in one's lies. 'In fact,' Gessen explains, 'the ability to change his story at will is a demonstration of power.'[33]

The ultimate form of such lying is the Big Lie – a propaganda technique Adolf Hitler described in *Mein Kampf*.[34] This is an assertion so grotesque that people presume there must be some truth to it – because surely no one would dare make up something so brazen. As Hitler wrote, '[The masses] more easily fall victim to a big lie than to a little one. Such a falsehood will never enter their heads, and they will not be able to believe in the possibility of such monstrous effrontery and infamous misrepresentation in others; yes, even when enlightened on the subject... Therefore, something of even the most insolent lie will always remain and stick'[35]

Victimhood

Every fascist claims that their own group is the victim of a conspiracy or a plot. An example of such a conspiracy theory is the 'Great Replacement' or 'white genocide': the idea that white people are deliberately being replaced by groups who are considered alien and hostile. Conspiracies like this hinge on 'outsiders' posing an existential threat in concert with 'elites' plotting to destroy the nation. 'This works with almost any combination of enemies,' Timothy Snyder explains. 'It can be a conspiracy of deep-state politicians to kidnap babies, or a conspiracy of Jews to corrupt women.'[36]

Hitler invoked an antisemitic conspiracy theory along these lines: Jews were secretly plotting world domination, he claimed, and there was a calculated plan for 'flooding our homeland by those of foreign blood and race'.[37] And so Jews were 'poisoning the blood' of the German nation, with the 'clear aim of... throwing it down from its cultural and political height, and himself rising to be its master'.[38] Marxism, Hitler believed, was but a tool in service of this goal.

Hitler's Big Lie fanned existing widespread grievances over Germany's defeat in World War I, and weaponized the popular stab-in-the-back-myth: the belief that the German empire had not been defeated on the battlefield, but rather double-crossed by its Jewish and leftist 'enemies' at home. Together, these narratives of victimhood and betrayal culminated in the claim that only through extermination could this existential threat be halted.

Hierarchy

Every fascist establishes a new social order based on claims about who is entitled to human dignity and who is not. The rights of minorities are dismantled, and people are persecuted not for what they do, but for who they are.

Those who benefit from this new ranking distrust those who speak out against it. An appeal to equal rights and equality becomes suspect and subversive. A mob of the meek helps to uphold the new order out of fear they themselves will be targeted.

Sexual anxiety

Every fascist defends rigid gender roles as a pillar of their power and as a cornerstone of the social hierarchy. Just as most leaders are portrayed as the 'father of the nation', men are seen as the natural head of the family – which is how fascists believe it should be. The masculinity of this leadership is vigorous and violent. Gender diversity is thus portrayed as a threat to this supposedly natural order.

When traditional male roles are put under pressure, fascist leaders hit back by pinpointing scapegoats: purveyors of 'gender ideology', or 'foreigners out to rape our women'. Women, meanwhile, are mainly supposed to have lots of (white) babies and thus strengthen the dominant group's position.

This is why Mussolini waged his economic 'Battle for Births', including publicised award ceremonies for especially fertile women and higher taxes for single men over the age of twenty-five. Terms like 'contraception' and 'abortion' were put on a list of words banned in the Italian press. [39]

Productivity

Every fascist divides people into 'hard-working citizens' and 'disposable freeloaders'. That division fuels the idea that their opponents are inferior and lazy by nature, and therefore don't deserve a proper place in society.

This idea creates yet another fault line in society. Hard-working citizens are necessary; the others – the intellectual elite, 'lazy' civil servants, people on welfare or with disabilities – are superfluous. *Arbeit macht frei*, as the Nazis inscribed on the gates of hell.

But that idealized work ethic is a smokescreen – fascists aren't really interested in changing the relations of production.[40] Any promise that the position of 'hard-working citizen' will improve one's lot is broken almost immediately. Business elites who fall into step with the regime get even richer, and the poor get even poorer. Hitler's Third Reich functioned as a predatory state, with corruption as its lubricant.[41] Hitler himself soon accumulated exorbitant personal wealth.[42]

The urban-rural divide

Every fascist pits cities against heartland, building on the idea that productive, honest work is essential to the nation's cultural restoration. The countryside becomes a symbol for virtuous, industrious, traditional people, whereas cities are depicted as needing to be purged of criminals and leftist work-shy scum and their depraved ideas about gender, diversity and inclusion.

According to the Nazis, for example, farmers were 'the main bearers of a healthy folkish heredity, the fountain of youth of the people and the backbone of military power'.[43]

Law and order

Every fascist transforms the law into a weapon with which to destroy their opponents. While placing themselves above the law and rewarding loyalists with impunity, the fascist uses the power of the law to punish those they designate 'criminals' without a fair trial. The leader embodies the people, and the people – i.e. the leader – are always right. This is how the fascist destroys the rule of law in the name of the law itself – without formally abolishing it.

Mussolini did this by incorporating the bar association. Lawyers were forced to uphold 'fascist justice', and so working with 'anti-fascists' in cases against loyal party members was out of the question.[44] Hitler for his part had an uncanny ability to identify 'the potential weakness inherent in every formal form of law', his legal adviser Hans Frank said.[45]

As soon as 'enemies' at home and abroad are seen as threats to national security, the fascist deploys all the state's resources – treasury, police, military, and security services – to persecute domestic enemies and challenge those abroad. They glorify violence as a source of power, security and peace – all for the greater honour and glory of the nation, i.e. themselves.

Recognizing contemporary fascism

So there it is: the fascists' playbook. This is how stoking discontent can result in an openly fascist regime.

Even though the steps are familiar and predictable, calling fascism 'fascism' at an early stage still meets resistance. The term immediately brings up images that are engraved in our collective memory: that little moustache, ecstatic crowds, Hitler salutes, brownshirts, Blackshirts, swastikas, paramilitary squads, and world war. And everyone knows the horrific consequences: the murder of 6 million Jews. That's fascism in its most radicalized form – its final, annihilatory stage.

That history makes us vigilant: no one wants to go back to that – not even, I suppose, the politicians now coming to power using fascist strategies. But that's precisely what's so insidious. As long as we continue to measure fascism against the Nazis, we miss what is going on right before our eyes: a politics built on hatred, enmity and dehumanization; a politics violently depriv- ing certain groups of their rights; a politics stripping society of the ability to think independently and of the possibility of public debate; a politics pairing the radicalization of the masses with an anti-democratic tyranny of the majority.

The differences from the past are real, but the pattern is clear. Today's far-right politicians mix the strategies of historical fascism with a post-war populism that has been firmly anchored in democracies worldwide.

This creates a new type of authoritarian leader, as historian Federico Finchelstein explains: the 'wannabe fascist' who draws from the playbook of historical fascism and undermines democracy from within by peddling racist lies and twisting the rule of law. Unlike full-fledged historical fascism, the aspiring fascists have 'not yet descended into dictatorship and [have] not fully relied on terror to monopolize violence and use it without restraint'.[46] But what starts with political leaders mobilizing the emotions of 'the people' against other groups in society can lead to the end of democracy as we know it. There's another crucial difference, however: thanks to history, we know how fascism develops and how we can protect democracy against it.

That knowledge can serve as a shield. We'd be crazy not to use it.

PART 2

Today's fascism

I know you want to free Palestine, free Congo, free Sudan, free Iran – it's a new one every week.

Free Europe! Free Europe from right-wing extremism, from fascism, from racism.

– Seun Kuti, Nigerian musician, Glastonbury Festival 2025

2. Fascism has a new face: the Trump regime

Look at the United States through the lens of fascism, and what at first appears a jumble of scandals, megalomania and mismanagement quickly reveals itself as a clear and persistent pattern in which the ten instruments of fascism coalesce. You can see Trump's fascist regime emerging in real time.

Robert Paxton, one of the great scholars of fascism, also came to recognize this pattern. At first, he refused to interpret the developments during Trump's first presidential term as overt fascism. But when he saw Trump supporters violently storm the Capitol on 6 January 2021, he changed his mind.[1] 'It's the real thing. It really is,' Paxton told *The New York Times*.[2]

How Trump uses the ten instruments of fascism

Like the fascists of old, Trump is employing the ten instruments of fascism. He, too, peddles a myth: that the once-great United States is being destroyed by 'criminal illegal aliens', who are 'poisoning the blood of the country',[3] conspiring with 'corrupt globalist elites'. His Make America Great Again slogan promises to put

America first, supposedly by returning to an era in which oil barons could drill wherever they wanted, no one was whining about climate change and white men were still undisputedly in charge.

Trump, too, floods the public discourse with lies. He told his first lie as president on day one, exaggerating the size of the crowd at his inauguration. In that first term, 30,572 equally demonstrable lies would follow – the *Washington Post* was counting.[4] And he has kept lying in his second term: Trump blamed a plane crash on diversity programmes,[5] and falsely accused schools of gender-confirmation surgeries on kids,[6] migrants of eating 'American' pets,[7] Ukraine of starting the war with Russia,[8] and so on. He spreads these falsehoods through executive orders, speeches and press briefings, but above all through his own social media platform – or rather, propaganda channel – Truth Social.

Trump, too, harasses and threatens independent thinkers – journalists, above all – on an almost daily basis. According to Trump, they are an enemy of the people. He scrapped funding for independent media,[9] restricted access to the White House for mainstream media outlets like the *New York Times*, *Politico* and the Associated Press, and made room for more ideologically like-minded influencers.[10] The Pentagon followed suit, welcoming a new wave of Trump-friendly reporters, taking the place of the journalists who left en masse in protest against being censored.[11]

Trump blackmails universities[12] and takes over important cultural institutions like museums,[13] which he has called the 'the last remaining segment of "WOKE"'.[14] When ultraconservative activist Charlie Kirk was murdered, he went even further. He claimed that radical left-wing rhetoric was directly responsible for 'the terrorism that we're seeing in our country today',[15] and he declared Antifa a terrorist organization.[16] Several media figures were suspended or fired over critical comments about Kirk's ideas.[17] The result: a culture of fear, self-censorship and, ultimately, the end of any kind of shared truth.

Trump, too, sees plots against the nation everywhere.[18] He called migrants 'garbage'[19] and an 'invasion poisoning the blood of our country'.[20] He launched a manhunt for the estimated 11 million undocumented people in the US.[21] Anything goes: using AI surveillance tools, Immigration and Customs Enforcement (ICE) can track immigrants and select them for deportation almost in real time.[22] Trump has not only tasked immigration agents to do this, but also government employees from other agencies, as well as 'other individuals'. Anyone who doesn't 'self-deport' voluntarily will be removed by force – 'in a place and manner solely of our discretion'.[23] The residency status of people from countries like Afghanistan and Somalia is being reviewed, and Trump openly talks about wanting to strip American citizenship from those who 'undermine domestic tranquillity' and deport any 'Foreign National' who is 'non-compatible with Western Civilization'.[24] Trump freed up an astronomical $175 billion for this operation, at the expense of the budget for Medicaid and SNAP, the federal food assistance programme.[25] White South Africans, meanwhile, were welcomed in the United States as people fleeing an alleged 'white genocide', turning the Great Replacement conspiracy theory into policy.[26]

Trump, too, claims there is a vast conspiracy by the 'globalist elite' abroad, in this case deliberately victimizing the United States and 'Western, Christian civilization' in general. This has led him to undermine the international rules-based order to an unprecedented extent.[27] One of the main culprits, in his eyes, is the European Union, whose actions amount to 'civilizational erasure'.[28]

Trump openly supports European opposition parties seeking to weaken the EU,[29] threatens to appropriate territory from (former?) allies[30] and blackmails NATO countries into buying more American arms. He's blocked the International Criminal Court with sanctions,[31] withdrawn from sixty-six international organizations and treaties,[32] and ceased funding what he calls 'radical left lunatics'[33] through the 'criminal organization' (in Elon Musk's words) USAID, the government agency for international development cooperation and humanitarian aid.

Humanitarian assistance is at odds with the main goal of Trump's foreign policy: profit. The start of his trade war was celebrated as 'Liberation Day' – and as an opportunity for MAGA-friendly billionaires to make a quick buck.[34] Even the genocide against the Palestinians seems to be treated as a potentially profitable real-estate project – the value of a strip of land on the Mediterranean outweighing the lives that would have to be wiped out to take it. Meanwhile, as the self-proclaimed 'President of Peace',[35] in 2025 Trump let himself be awarded the inaugural FIFA Peace Prize, created for the occasion, and accepted a second-hand Nobel Peace Prize from the actual winner[36] – despite the fact that the US bombed at least seven countries that year,[37] not to mention the subsequent capture of the Venezuelan president Nicolás Maduro and the illegal US strikes on Iran.

Trump, too, is establishing a new social hierarchy, including tip lines for civil servants, schools and citizens to report those who allegedly threaten it: 'woke culture warriors'[38] and immigrants.[39] This social order also enforces rigid gender roles. Trump has banned trans people from the military, sports and public life, while also erasing words like 'gender', 'feminism' and 'equality' from all government communications.[40] Beauty ideals have followed suit – the so-called Mar-a-Lago face, a term referencing MAGA women's plastic-surgery rictus, sets the standard, alongside strict new appearance codes for military personnel. He has talked about a 'National Medal of Motherhood' for prolific mothers, and cash bonuses for producing more 'American' children.[41] This is because, as can be read in his national security strategy, 'growing numbers of strong, traditional families that raise healthy children' are needed for 'the restoration and reinvigoration of American spiritual and cultural health, without which long-term security is impossible'.[42]

Trump, too, divides people into 'geniuses' and 'dummies', 'winners' and 'losers'. According to him, his friends in tech have 'a high IQ', while he often calls his opponents 'low-IQ individuals'.[43] He wants a 'gainfully employed citizenry… who take satisfaction from knowing that their work is essential to the prosperity of our nation'.[44] Considered inessential: the estimated 121,000 civil servants fired by Elon Musk's Department of Government Efficiency (DOGE)[45] for being 'ideologically corrupted'[46] or, according to Musk, replaceable by chatbots.[47]

Trump, too, garnered massive support in rural areas, with his promise to deal with 'radicalized environmentalists'[48] and – with the help of federal funds – transform progressive 'pro-crime' sanctuary cities such as Washington, DC, into MAGA strongholds.[49] In August 2025, Trump put his plan into action, and the first armoured National Guard vehicles rolled into the capital as the DC police force was placed under federal control. He made it clear that this was just the beginning: Chicago, Trump shared on Truth Social, was about to find out why the Department of Defense was now 'called the Department of WAR'.[50] He presented his plan as a response to the 'violent gangs and bloodthirsty criminals' in supposedly lawless, Democrat-run cities – despite crime rates actually falling to all-time lows.[51] In practice, this amounted to both a federal seizure of power in opposition strongholds and additional manpower for immigration raids.[52]

Finally, Trump, too, is well on his way to turning the rule of law into a weapon with which to bludgeon his opponents.[53] He had tech billionaire Elon Musk take a chainsaw to the civil service, replaced women and people of colour in top management positions with white men,[54] fired independent experts[55] and demanded absolute loyalty from his officials.[56]

Trump has sanctioned law firms for representing clients critical of him or his cronies,[57] had a judge arrested and indicted for obstructing the US government,[58] and abused his legal authority to disappear immigrants and silence his critics.[59] As prescribed in the national security memorandum NSPM-7 on domestic terrorism, anyone Trump considers anti-American, anti-capitalist or anti-Christian, or who has 'extremist' ideas about migration, race and gender – lumped together under the label of 'anti-fascist'– is the target of investigation and prosecution.[60]

At this point, Trump unequivocally labels his political opposition 'the enemy from within'[61] – declaring that 'the greatest enemy America has is the Radical Left, Highly Incompetent, Democrat Party'.[62] He has threatened to use the army against them and floated using 'dangerous' liberal cities as 'training grounds' for those types of operations.[63] And when Democrats called on active service members to refuse such – unconstitutional – orders, he accused them of 'SEDITIOUS BEHAVIOR, punishable by DEATH'.[64]

Trump himself is above the law, he believes. As he himself posted: 'He who saves his Country does not violate any Law.'[65]

Donald Trump's Big Lie: 'Stop the steal'

And then, again straight from the fascist playbook, there's Trump's Big Lie: the 'stolen' 2020 presidential elections.

By then, the warning signals were already loud and clear. They became deafening after Trump lost to Joe Biden and made a claim so outrageous that it inevitably left its mark: that a conspiracy of 'left lunatics, Venezuela and China' had committed electoral fraud and thus stolen Trump's presidency. He then mobilized a broad mass movement that stormed the Capitol, home to the US Congress, to 'stop the steal'.[66] Trump, however, blamed the day's violence on 'the corrupt FBI', 'Antifa terrorists' and Nancy Pelosi, then Speaker of the House of Representatives.[67]

He dismissed the subsequent probe into his role in the attack as sheer abuse of power by the 'deep state', an alleged shadow network of officials, judges and security services. According to Trump, the Justice Department was being weaponized – against him, but primarily against the nation: 'In the end, they're not coming after me. They're coming after you – and I'm just standing in their way.'[68]

This puts a perfectly twenty-first-century twist on the stab-in-the-back myth so famously employed by the Nazis: Trump wasn't defeated at the polls, but by traitors at home who wanted to poison the nation by letting in migrants.[69] Existential threat: check. Conspiracy of domestic elites: check.

Four years later, on the first day of his second term, Trump pardoned nearly 1,600 convicted Capitol-stormers – whom he renamed 'January 6 hostages'. Among them were the leaders of far-right militias like the Proud Boys and Oath Keepers. In doing so, he not only excused them but also their violent, anti-democratic methods. This earned him a loyal band of armed thugs, who know they have Trump to thank for their freedom and who openly profess to be out for revenge.[70]

And perhaps most importantly: Trump got away with it. He faced next to no consequences, and even took action against those involved in his prosecution.[71] 'That made the Big Lie true, in a fascist sense,' says Timothy Snyder. 'His de-facto impunity and then de-jure immunity also generated a sense of the untouchable, the heroic.'[72]

Trump supporters even found proof of Trump's inviolability – as did Trump himself – in the failed attempt on his life during his 2024 election campaign. The bullet, they believed, was narrowly averted by 'divine intervention'.[73] He was seen no longer as simply an elected leader, but as someone chosen by a higher power to save the nation.

But just as it's a fallacy to ascribe some divine mandate to Trump, it's too simplistic to see him as the sole explanation for how things got to this point.

Deep American roots

The Trump regime is not a deviation from the course of American history, but a direct product of it. Each country gets its own fascism; the United States got Trumpism, a fascism of the purest American pedigree.[74] Trump's fascism has a 'much more solid social base', Robert Paxton says, and that's something 'neither Hitler nor Mussolini would have had'.[75]

The Trump regime has evolved from the historical foundations of slavery and the racist Jim Crow laws that robbed Black Americans of their basic constitutional rights at the end of the nineteenth century (this form of legalized segregation in turn inspired Hitler's Nuremberg race laws, which laid the groundwork for the Holocaust). Black Americans – along with Native Americans, Latinos, and Muslims – will be the first to point out that a politics of exclusion and violence in the US is nothing new. It's been around for centuries.

The Trump regime is made up of the socio-economic debris of the American Dream, under which poverty is considered a personal failure and individual success always comes at others' expense. It is assembled from repurposed legislative rubble left over from the War on Terror, and brought to life by tech oligarchs like Elon Musk and Mark Zuckerberg, whose algorithms cut up the public sphere into bite-sized pieces, then feed them to trolls and conspiracy theorists.

And the Trump regime could take root and grow because of a noxious yet fertile mix of existential threats, like the depletion of the planet, the climate crisis, the Covid pandemic, and a technology revolution that would make people redundant.[76] The very richest individuals on earth then hot-housed Trumpism into maturity by throwing the money at it that was needed to regain the White House. [77]

Moreover, Trump's regime not only relies on an alliance of MAGA demagogues and far-right conspiracy theorists; it is a broad coalition whose members have found common ground in their support for Trump. Trump is a political ringleader – he mobilizes the masses, polarizes public debate and demolishes institutions – but it is the ultraconservatives who cooked up the strategy for his seizure of power, and it is Silicon Valley that has provided the digital infrastructure.

For decades, ultraconservative forces were working behind the scenes on a detailed plan to transform the United States into an authoritarian, Christian, white ethno-state – eventually formalized as Project 2025. Developed by the ultraconservative think tank the Heritage Foundation, it serves as a blueprint for dismantling the liberal-democratic rule of law. The avalanche of executive orders, the politicization of departments and agencies, the mass deportation of migrants and the use of trade policy as a geopolitical weapon – these were all measures waiting for the right president to enter the White House. That happened in 2016, with Donald J. Trump.

Now, contributors to this plan hold key government positions. Russell Vought heads the Office of Management and Budget, Stephen Miller is one of Trump's primary advisers, Tom Homan became 'border czar',[78] John Ratcliffe heads the CIA, and Peter Navarro is in charge of trade policy. Their success is measurable: by the end of 2025, it was estimated that half of Project 2025 had already been implemented.[79]

Then there are the tech billionaires. They have rallied behind Trump with two strategic goals: deregulating Big Tech and capturing the entire infrastructure of the American state. As Francesca Bria, associate professor of technology and innovation policy at University College London, put it: 'Silicon Valley isn't building apps anymore. It's building empires.'[80] And if it is up to the world's wealthiest, these empires will certainly not be democratic. Peter Thiel, founder of Palantir Technologies and mentor and financier to US vice president J. D. Vance, has openly stated that he no longer believes 'freedom and democracy are compatible'.[81] Friend and inspiration to Vance, Curtis Yarvin, a blogger serving as Silicon Valley's house philosopher, dreams aloud of a state led by a CEO-in-chief, transforming the government into 'a heavily-armed, ultra-profitable corporation'.[82] And tech-venture capitalist Marc Andreessen preaches that unrestrained artificial intelligence can elevate humanity to a 'superman'.[83]

In exchange for their support, these men have been given unprecedented access to power. They have raked in contracts worth billions, taken up strategic positions within the White House, and gained control of critical military infrastructure. Some Silicon Valley executives were even sworn in as lieutenant colonels in the US Army.[84] With his demolition team, DOGE, Elon Musk took over government buildings and digital databases, firing thousands of civil servants. At the same time, swathes of data were copied and exploited on a massive scale: now, the personal data of millions of citizens is likely to have been aggregated in central databases. In practice, this has amounted to a digital coup.[85] As Bria aptly typifies it: 'Unlike old authoritarianism built on fear and force, this new system rules through code, capital, and infrastructure – making resistance feel architecturally impossible.'[86]

As Trump whips up the MAGA movement, ultraconservatives and tech billionaires have each backed his authoritarian power grab in their own way. Despite their differences, they share a hierarchical view of humanity and the conviction that building a 'better' future is only possible on the ashes of liberal democracy.[87]

This echoes Robert Paxton's characterization of fascist regimes as a polycracy: an unstable pact in which multiple powers coexist, temporarily cooperate and constantly compete. Paxton warns that this kind of instability can have a radicalizing effect on the leader of a fascist regime: 'He can never lean back; he has to keep feeding the masses the story that he's saving the country from the "enemy".'[88] Fail to do so and the fascist movement disintegrates, turning into an 'ordinary' authoritarian regime. So far, Trump has not leaned back.

Moderate politicians gave Trump free rein

Moderate politicians – from progressive to conservative – should have seen Trump's seizure of power coming from miles away. The signs were omnipresent: the absurd lies, the overt racism, the Capitol attack, the threats against political opponents, the open fantasies about abolishing democracy, Project 2025. These politicians failed in their core task to protect democracy against this kind of constitutional pyromania. According to political scientists Steven Levitsky and Daniel Ziblatt, the authors of *How Democracies Die* (2018), this failure to act was due to the unfounded idea that democratic elections keep anti-democrats out.[89]

Other political lines of defence also went unused, they say: Republicans could have expelled Trump from the party because of his undemocratic behaviour, but they either capitulated or joined his cause. Congress could have used its constitutional right to exclude Trump from future elections because of his role in the storming of the Capitol, but failed to do so. And neither moderate Republicans nor Democrats were willing to put aside their party interests to join forces against Trump.[90]

And so the door swung wide open for the next stage of Trump's power grab. On his return to the White House, he unleashed an avalanche of executive orders, seizing as much executive power as possible and largely sidelining Congress.[91] He then turned on the judiciary. The courts can barely keep up with Trump's torrent of unconstitutional acts – after all, carefully conducted legal proceedings take time. Even so, federal judges have already blocked some 150 policies of his administration since Trump took office for his second term.[92]

Trump's legal team invariably responds to these verdicts with legal loopholes to undermine those rulings, right up to the Supreme Court. In June 2025, that court limited – by a narrow majority – the power of federal judges to stop presidential executive orders. An 'existential threat to the rule of law', one of the dissenting judges called it.[93] Countervailing legal power is thus shifting to the Supreme Court, where the so-called shadow docket plays an increasingly important role. This emergency docket was intended for exceptional and temporary interventions, but it has become a common route for the White House to suspend or neutralize lower court rulings. Almost nine times out of ten, the temporary rulings resulting from this emergency procedure are in favour of the White House.[94] The damage caused is often irreversible.[95]

The battle with the judiciary escalated when Trump used the 1798 Alien Enemies Act to take a seemingly random group of immigrants and send them – without a fair trial and in violation of a court order – to a notorious prison in El Salvador to disappear.[96] When the Supreme Court then ordered the return of one of the men, Kilmar Ábrego García, Trump refused.[97]

Instead, Trump launched a public smear campaign, sharing a digitally manipulated photo of Ábrego García's tattooed hands as supposed proof he was a member of the MS-13 gang[98] – yet Ábrego García had no criminal record. Only once the controversy about his deportation had grown too loud did the government open a criminal investigation, eventually returning Ábrego García to the

US. On arrival, he faced a new cobbled-together charge of human trafficking, based on dubious testimony.[99]

The authorities swore that Ábrego García 'would never walk free on US soil' but showed little interest in bringing him to trial.[100] He was detained, released and detained again. But he wasn't brought to trial, nor was he presented with a final order of removal.

As a result, a judge ruled in December 2025 that Ábrego García had been imprisoned 'without lawful authority', so he was set free – once again. Her scathing verdict stated that the White House had 'affirmatively misled' the court and that 'whatever purpose was behind his detention, it was not for the "basic purpose" of timely third-country removal'.[101] The White House press secretary lashed out at the judge, saying that the administration opposed 'this activism from a judge who is really acting as a judicial activist, which unfortunately we have seen in many cases across the country'.[102]

Promising national rebirth. Abusing laws. Deciding who is a criminal on a whim. Declaring enemies and making them disappear. Bypassing courts with sloppy indictments. *This* is fascism. This is how the rule of law is demolished in the name of the law.

Paramilitary thugs

Meanwhile, Trump has been building his fascist regime virtually unhindered, transforming Immigration and Customs Enforcement into a paramilitary band of thugs.

ICE's budget has been increased so much that it now exceeds the budgets of all the other police and security agencies combined.[103] They recruit new personnel with bonuses[104] and promotional videos full of references to Nazism and white Christian nationalism.[105] This is how they have more than doubled their staff. There's no age limit and little selection or training, but recruits are given heavy weaponry, advanced surveillance tools, extensive powers, and instructions from the White House that they can operate with impunity.[106]

And they do. 2025 went down as ICE's deadliest year in two decades: thirty-two people died in custody.[107] ICE operations are now designed not only to round up as many people with a migration background as possible, but also to terrorize anyone who dares to disagree. In early 2026, this became terrifyingly clear in Minneapolis, a decidedly anti-Trump city. Federal forces rounded up more than 4,000 people, wrenching waiters from their work,[108] using pre-schoolers as bait,[109] and dragging people out of their houses in nothing but their underwear.[110]

Renée Good, an American poet trying to protect her neighbours from this violence, was killed in her car by an ICE agent as she tried to drive away. 'That's fine, dude, I'm not mad at you' were the last words she said to him. 'Fucking bitch,' the ICE agent shouted after her as her car crashed into a parked vehicle at the side of the road.[111]

A few weeks later, Alex Pretti, another US citizen and a nurse, was shot ten times by a Border Patrol agent as he was on his knees trying to protect a woman from tear gas. 'Boo hoo,' one of the other officers shouted at the shocked crowd.[112]

'What I've seen here is what I've seen there,' the city's emergency management director Rachel Sayre said, comparing the events in Minneapolis to conflict zones in

Yemen, Haiti, Syria, Iraq and Ukraine.[113] Or, in the words of one of the ICE agents filmed on the street: 'It's like *Call of Duty*. So cool, huh?'[114]

At least as important is the regime's rhetoric around ICE's actions. The Trump administration blames the violence and the deaths of Good and Pretti on the 'radical left' and the 'fake media', which supposedly radicalized these people into 'domestic terrorists' against whom ICE agents had merely been defending themselves.[115] Framing anti-ICE protesters as 'terrorists' traces back to presidential memo NSPM-7, in which 'extremism on migration' is designated a hallmark of 'domestic terrorism'.[116] What is more: the White House made this claim, *despite video evidence of the killings proving otherwise.* Remember the function of the fascist lie: it does not ask people to believe something new, but to disbelieve what they can see with their own eyes – testing the loyalty of sycophants, stoking hatred among supporters, and staging power as spectacle.

So the White House pledges its full support to ICE based on a demonstrable lie and under the motto 'Blessed are the peacemakers'.[117] But on the streets, other slogans can be heard: 'ICE out for Good' and 'A Pretti Good reason for a national strike'. And the resistance to ICE's terror continues, sometimes at a high personal cost. Protesters risk tear gas, violence, arrest and even death in their attempts to stop what Trump has started. This resistance is about much more than harsh deportation policies. It is a battle for the liberal democracy of the United States – one of the oldest and most robust democracies in the world.

The question is: can this resistance stop Trump?

The road to dictatorship

During a television interview in the spring of 2025, Trump was asked: 'Don't you need to uphold the Constitution of the United States as president?'

He replied, 'I don't know.'[118]

Rounding up people, killing citizens, sidestepping courts, silencing friends and foes alike – it all serves as a test. It's not about what Trump is legally *allowed* to do, but what he can get away with. Whether he really is above the law.[119] '"If we can defy this, then we're home free," is the thinking,' warns former FBI agent and Yale assistant dean Asha Rangappa.[120] Then it will be up to Trump to determine who is a criminal and how they should be punished. And judges have no means of enforcing their rulings – that power lies with the executive branch. In other words, with Trump.

By his own account, Trump now has far more power than during his first term. 'The first time, I had two things to do – run the country and survive; I had all these crooked guys,' he told the *Atlantic* in April 2025. 'And the second time, I run the country and the world.'[121] Less than a year later, he stated that he himself was the only limit to his global power: 'My own morality. My own mind. It's the only thing that can stop me.'[122] And if anyone had any doubts about what he meant by that, at the 2026 World Economic Forum in Davos he spelled it out: 'I am a dictator. But sometimes, you need a dictator.'[123]

There is no question about where this is headed, if it were up to Trump: his unbridled power. Trump's contempt for elections has been plain since his coup attempt in 2021, after he claimed the presidential election the previous year had been 'stolen'. In early 2026, he even published this false claim on the White House website[124] and is having the FBI investigate it again – though it has long since been debunked.

That Big Lie serves as a pretext to seize control of the midterm elections in November 2026, in order to consolidate his power. Under the guise of protecting electoral integrity, he stated he wanted to nationalize them, implying that he wants to take power away from state governments that are constitutionally in charge of regulating elections.[125] He also said: 'We shouldn't even have an election.'[126]

By the end of 2025, preparations for manipulating these midterm elections were already in full swing: from attempts to restrict mail-in voting and ban voting machines, to redrawing districts to the Republicans' advantage, creating a central voter database with sensitive personal data, and trying to impose new ID requirements for voters – which could block millions of Americans from voting.[127]

It could hardly be clearer: Trump does not intend to accept a Republican loss in the midterms, or any loss at all. He aims to build a regime that can survive him. They're already selling a new hat: Trump 2028.

Can Trumpism be stopped?

Congress still has one emergency brake: it can remove Trump from the presidency through an impeachment procedure. However, with a Republican majority behind him, that option doesn't stand a chance.[128] Trump already shared how he'll react to any attempt at impeachment: 'These Radical Left Lunatics are into the "Impeachment thing" again... Perhaps we should start playing this game on them, and expel Democrats.'[129]

If judges, senators and representatives can barely take a stand, large-scale social mobilization is the only option left. People from all walks of life need to join forces to hold the line and stop Trump. 'It's an all-hands-on-deck moment,' civil rights activist Carol Rose says. 'And we can't afford to say "well, we're gonna leave it to the courts, we're gonna leave it to the journalists, we're gonna leave it to the protestors."' She's convinced Trump can only be stopped if people join forces. 'Every one of us has to be in this fight right now!'[130]

That fight is spreading, the resistance is growing, and support for Trump's methods is declining.[131] In all fifty states, judges, lawyers, journalists, protesters and universities are pushing back. In all fifty states, in protests that are among the largest in US history, millions of Americans have taken to the streets to protest Trump's authoritarianism.[132]

Even within the MAGA movement, the first clear fault lines are showing. And Trump's initial refusal to disclose the Epstein files has threatened to turn those fault lines into a rupture. The strikes on Iran have deepened them further: a significant minority of Republicans disapprove of how Trump is handling the war.[133]

Trump, however, does not tolerate criticism, let alone resistance. He hits back hard, and with much spectacle.[134] In Los Angeles, for example, he – illegally, a judge later ruled[135] – sent in 2,000 members of the National Guard, against the express wish of Democratic governor Gavin Newsom, who concluded 'democracy is under assault before our eyes'.[136] Dozens of people were arrested at the No Kings protests in early June 2025, including an eighty-seven-year-old veteran in a wheelchair.[137] After that, several Democrat officials were very publicly handcuffed, arrested or charged for asking questions about the deportation of migrants.[138]

Meanwhile, Trump appointed conservative activist and lawyer Ed Martin, who previously helped organize the 'Stop the Steal' protests and served as an attorney for January 6 defendants, as the Justice Department's 'weaponization czar'. His explicit mission: to detect and punish political opponents.

Judges, elected officials and protesters have all learned that opposition to Trump carries a real risk. His earlier threats of 'retribution'[139] have become standard practice.[140]

Or, as the White House prefers to picture it: 'A golden age [is] just getting started.'

3. Fascist patterns in Europe today

Europe may differ from the United States in a multitude of ways, but they have one thing in common: they are not immune to the pull of fascism. Not in the past, and not now.

'Trumpism is part of a twenty-first-century global trend towards autocracy that has reformulated the history of populism, turning it into wannabe fascism,' says Federico Finchelstein.[1] Far-right politicians in Europe have gained influence in recent years by digging up a hate many hoped was dead and buried. They have stoked a loathing for 'wokeism' and 'gender theory', 'illegal foreign criminals', 'fascist liberals' and the 'parasitic press', to name just a few. Backed and emboldened by Donald Trump, these populist movements are starting to display openly fascist traits.

Take the leader of Alternative for Germany (AfD), Alice Weidel, who was openly endorsed by Trump and his cronies during her 2025 election campaign.[2] She promised mass deportations and encouraged crowds chanting *'Alice für Deutschland'* – echoing *Alles für Deutschland*, the banned Nazi battle cry dating back to 1920s. The AfD went on to become the second-largest party in the country.

Or the Italian prime minister Giorgia Meloni of the Brothers of Italy party, who joined forces with Trump 'to make the West great again'.[3] Meloni claims the Italian population is being 'ethnically replaced' by 'African boat refugees',[4] and that mass immigration is 'an instrument in the hands of big great powers.'[5] Like Mussolini a hundred years ago, she wants Italian women to bear more children,[6] while in practice excluding same-sex couples from starting families.[7] Meanwhile, her government – following the US example – has been looking for ways to circumvent EU legislation and treaties in order to cage migrants in a prison in Albania, outside the European Union and out of sight of journalists.[8]

Or French National Rally leader Marine Le Pen – who, just like Trump, called the criminal conviction barring her from the next elections 'an attack on democracy'.[9] The same Marine Le Pen who wants to bar people without a French passport – 'illegal migrants, delinquents and foreign criminals', as she calls them – from housing and social provisions,[10] shut down mosques,[11] and use referenda to pit the 'will of the people' against the courts.[12]

And don't forget former Hungarian prime minister Viktor Orbán. He and his party, Fidesz, curtailed the power of judges and the independence of universities and the media to such a degree that Hungary is now internationally regarded as a textbook example of democracy's decay. To supposedly protect children from the display or discussion of homosexuality, he banned the sale of unwrapped children's books featuring LGBTQI+ themes to minors. It wasn't long before he banned Budapest Pride too.[13] Orbán sought to eliminate the 'shadow army' of 'politicians, judges, journalists, pseudo-NGOs and political activists'. To do so, he reached for a foreign-agent bill designed to dismantle the 'financial machine' that paid for this alleged shadow army with 'corrupt dollars'.[14]

Hold these politicians up to the fascist playbook, and everything gets ticked off. Mythic past: check. Propaganda: check. Attacking journalists: check. Sexual anxiety: check. Victimhood: check. Weaponizing law and order: check, check, check.

Far-right parties are attracting more and more voters with this strategy. For the first time in modern history, these parties have jointly won a greater share of the vote in European countries than conservative or social democratic movements.[15] In several countries, far-right parties are well represented in the government. Support has grown significantly in countries such as Germany, France and the Netherlands.

Meanwhile, liberal democracy is rapidly backsliding across the continent, according to V-Dem, one of the leading global monitors of democracy.[16] In Italy, Slovakia, Slovenia, Greece, Croatia and Romania, governments are actively undermining the rule of law and curtailing press freedoms. These countries are now classified as 'autocratizing states'. In the UK, deteriorating academic and cultural freedoms and increasing media self-censorship have landed the country on the same V-Dem list of 'autocratizers'. Hungary has passed that stage entirely, and is now classified as an electoral autocracy: a country that still holds elections but is governed as an autocracy.

European cooperation against the EU

Unlike the historical movements on which Robert Paxton based his insights, most of these far-right parties operate on a new playing field: the European Union. And all of them run up against the liberal international rules-based, legal order that emerged after World War II, with institutions like the United Nations, the World Health Organization and the World Trade Organization, alongside international trade agreements, courts and human rights treaties. This rules-based order serves as sturdy guardrails preventing national democracies from flying off the track.

Or, as the far right would say, as barriers that prevent them from – for example – mass-deporting refugees, criminalizing mosque attendance and banning abortion. Which explains why far-right parties, each with their own ultranationalist agenda, find common cause in their shared desire to once again position the European continent as the 'beacon of Christian culture' – and restore each country's national identity to its 'full glory'. In other words: to dismantle the European Union as we know it.

Following a historic win in the 2024 European elections, far-right parties are divided across three different political groups in the European Parliament: the European Conservatives and Reformists (including Meloni's Brothers of Italy), the Patriots for Europe (including Geert Wilders's PVV and Orbán's Fidesz)[17] and the Europe of Sovereign Nations (within which Alice Weidel's AfD is by far the biggest party).[18]

Together, these three groups hold over a quarter of the seats. They do not agree on everything by any means, but they do come together to stamp their mark on EU policies, often with support from the Christian Democrat European People's Party (EPP) and sometimes the Liberals.

The European Parliament voted, for example, to establish a controversial Scrutiny Working Group to probe the funding of non-governmental organizations (NGOs),[19] targeting a supposedly vast network of organizations allegedly advancing the European Commission's pro-climate and migration-friendly agenda.[20] It was a step akin to Orbán's proposed law on foreign agents that sought to silence his critics.

Meanwhile, the European Green Deal was watered down in a bid to head off criticism from far-right parties that knew how to channel farmers' discontent. Nature restoration ambitions, stricter emission standards and sustainable agriculture goals were scaled back or post-poned.[21] To top it all off, the Patriots for Europe, enabled by the Christian Democratic European People's Party, secured one of the most important climate positions in the European Parliament: lead negotiator for the EU's 2040 climate targets. By backing this, the EPP broke with the informal agreement between centre and left groups to keep the far right out of such positions of power.[22] It was but a prelude to closer political cooperation: in November 2025, the EPP formed a majority with the far-right block to water down legislation on human rights, sustainability, technology and privacy.[23]

And in March 2026, a coalition of the EPP and conserv-ative far-right groups adopted a reform of EU migration rules, effectively legalizing what had until then been illegal under European law: shipping migrants to third countries outside the EU.[24] Exactly what Giorgia Meloni already had been doing. By repeatedly praising the Italian prime minister's defiance of the law as a 'possible model' for future migration policy, EU Commission president Ursula von der Leyen (a member of the EPP) helped her blaze a trail for what has become the new normal.[25]

Due to the far right's systematic attacks on everything 'woke', 'green' or 'global', centrist parties routinely wash their hands in advance of themes such as diversity, inclusion and climate. As a result, the far right stamps a firmer mark on the EU's direction than their seat count and internal divisions would suggest.[26] Paxton's warning echoes: this is how the established elites help normalize the far right.

Another of Paxton's warnings also resonates here: 'We must spend as much time studying their indispensable allies and accomplices as we spend studying the fascist leaders.'[27] Every variation of fascism has rested on a shaky, opportunistic pact between far-right politicians and conservative or economic powers. Today, the far-right strives not only to undermine national democracies, but also to dismantle the EU and demolish the international rules-based order. It's only natural that the far right looks across borders to find friends.

If we are to understand how fascism works today, we need to understand its international network – the way it cooperates with all manner of groups globally, both within and outside the realm of politics. Politicians, think tanks, religious groups, media magnates, tech-utopians and billionaires who are sympathetic to the far right strengthen each other's scorn for multilateral institutions and agreements, work together on joint strategies to attack them, and adopt the same language and methods.

Step by step, they inflict irreversible damage on the guardrails of our political freedoms.

An international ecosystem united through hate

So who belongs to this network, and how do they support each other?

Far-right parties don't only join forces in the European Parliament. They also meet like-minded politicians, think tanks and media from Europe and further afield at annual conferences. An extensive data survey of these conferences revealed a 'startling – and strengthening – network of events and speakers that has helped spread a global pandemic of far-right extremism'.[28]

Europe is by far the prime location for this kind of conference, followed by the United States. The central hubs in what the study showed is now a truly transnational movement are the National Conservatism Conference, better known as NatCon, and the Conservative Political Action Conference, or CPAC. Beyond the endless speeches and networking events, these gatherings are where joint initiatives take shape.

At the April 2024 CPAC in Hungary, for example, a working group called 'Wokebusters' was announced – a sort of emergency hotline to warn members about the 'nefarious activity of progressive woke actors' – alongside a programme to bring far-right activists together.[29] At the following year's CPAC, again in Hungary, participants announced the 'Global Coalition against Globalism' – yes, that is actually what it was called.[30] It's always the same old tune: get rid of the 'Brussels' red tape, end mass immigration and stop the 'tyranny of liberal opinion'.

Someone who knows the groups in this network well is Jelle Postma. He has worked for not only the Dutch intelligence and security service (AIVD), but also for the United Nations and the Dutch National Coordinator for Security and Counterterrorism. He left the intelligence world to set up Justice for Prosperity, a foundation that researches how liberal democracies are being undermined in real time, putting his spycraft to work for the greater good.

In his office in Amsterdam, he explained to me how far-right parties fit into the broader transnational movement. 'Far-right leaders are only one of the players. They are part of an unholy alliance of ultraconservative think tanks, right-wing extremists and influencers, oligarchs, tech bosses and industrialists.'[31]

The alliance stretches from Europe to the US, from Russia to Latin America, from Africa to China. It's no secret, for example, that Russian president Vladimir Putin is seriously undermining Europe's stability through relentless disinformation campaigns, the sabotaging of critical infrastructure, a war of aggression in Ukraine, and the threat of hybrid warfare across the rest of Europe. 'It is a transnational ecosystem,' Postma told me, 'united by hatred and a shared ambition to gain power.'

Does this sound like a conspiracy? 'At times it does,' Postma admitted. 'Ultraconservatives have been working on this for decades. They are the brains behind the cooperation. Now that the right political players are in the right positions to turn these ideas into political action, they're seizing their chance.'

Even though each group in this transnational movement has its own agenda, they all unite against the 'global liberal elite' and the minorities that elite is protecting: migrants, LGBTQI+ communities – essentially, anyone who doesn't fit their nostalgic image of the so-called Judeo-Christian civilization. The goal: to undermine the international rules-based order[32] and its depraved 'liberal globalist' ideas.[33]

Fake news, court cases and disrupting the debate

To achieve this aim, these groups deploy a mix of disruption strategies that go beyond the political domain.[34] One way they do this is by spreading disinformation. Whether it's about 'criminal refugees', 'paedophile children's books', vaccinations, the nitrogen crisis or Covid, Postma says, the outrage is always stoked by the same online accounts.

Ultraconservative think tanks like the Polish Ordo Iuris are training lawyers to file court cases against activists and abortion doctors, and they back farmers protesting the European Green Deal.[35] Strategic litigation by this type of think tank led to a strict ban on abortion in Poland in 2021,[36] and contributed to removing the constitutional right to abortion in the United States the following year.[37]

They also teach like-minded NGO staff how to obtain certain privileges with international institutions, in order to influence the debate from within. Training material includes statements such as 'human rights, including dignity, life, and liberty, are constantly being challenged in the international arena, including by *human rights organizations and tribunals* [my italics]'.[38] It is an inversion tactic straight out of the fascist playbook: undermine human rights in the *name* of human rights.

And there are consequences. This is, for example, how organizations like Ordo Iuris prevented abortion from being recognized as a human right, and stopped references to women's reproductive and sexual rights from being included in the final report of the UN Commission on the Status of Women.[39]

Postma bases his insights on in-depth research. His team scours online platforms day in, day out – analysing huge quantities of data, collecting open-source intelligence and gathering information in the field. This allows them to track the key players, map their money flows and learn what plans are underway. The aim is to unravel this network and protect the people it affects.

But Postma is far from the only one keeping an eye on this growing cooperation, this 'ecosystem united by hate'. Catherine de Vries, professor of political science and president of the Institute for European Policymaking at Milan's Bocconi University, describes it as a 'motley crew of divergent interests that come together around a shared aversion to the liberal order'.

'Fascism was always transnational,' says Federico Finchelstein, who as well as authoring several books on fascism is the University in Exile Research Professor at the New School for Social Research, 'in the sense that fascist movements collaborated in their attack on universal liberal values. Today's increased collaboration marks a reconnection to this past, while the institutionalization of those values has intensified the transnational character of this new form of fascism.'[40]

To be clear: this is not a uniform, well-oiled, transnational fascist machine run by the Trumps of this world. Think of it instead as a loose web of authoritarian leaders

– like Trump, but also Vladimir Putin and Benjamin Netanyahu – as well as ultraconservative ideologists, far-right groups, influencers and business elites who, each for their own reasons, are helping pave the way for a successful fascist strategy in the US and Europe. It is an opportunistic and temporary pact of allies and accomplices on a global scale.

A new 'alliance for civilization'

With Trump's return to the White House, the European far right has a strong ally on the other side of the Atlantic. In February 2025, several of these politicians gathered in Madrid to celebrate the new Trump era under the motto 'Make Europe Great Again'.[41] Former Hungarian prime minister Viktor Orbán cheered Trump's re-election as a sign that far-right politicians across the world had gone from 'being heretics to mainstream'. And Geert Wilders, leader of the Dutch far-right Party for Freedom (PVV), declared in turn that 'Trump brought a message of hope'. As Finchelstein put it: 'Trump legitimizes and enables them all.'[42]

The Trump regime certainly shares their dislike of the European Union. In the same month as the Madrid gathering, US vice president J. D. Vance launched a fierce attack on Europe at the Munich Security Conference. 'The threat,' he declared, 'comes from within', because in his view European leaders were turning away from the most fundamental democratic values.[43]

Three months later, the White House further elaborated on this position in 'The Need for Civilizational Allies in Europe'.[44] This policy paper included statements such as: 'Europe has devolved into a hotbed of digital censorship, mass migration, restrictions on religious freedom… Our hope is that both Europe and the United States can recommit to our Western heritage, and that European nations will end the weaponization of government against those seeking to defend it.' At stake – the White House claimed – was nothing less than Western civilization.

In November 2025, all of this came together in the Trump administration's National Security Strategy. In this document, the White House coupled its domestic policy agenda for the 'reinvigoration of spiritual and cultural health' with an aggressive foreign policy aimed at fighting globalism, liberal values and multilateral institutions. The European Union, with its 'elite-driven, anti-democratic restrictions on core liberties', was designated the primary target.

Just as Hitler professed in *Mein Kampf* that France would become a 'European-African mulatto state… filled with a lower race gradually produced from continuous bastardization',[45] Washington claims that countries in Europe will soon become 'majority non-European' – as a result of EU policies that are allowing migration to get out of hand, driving down birth rates and, therefore, wiping out European civilization. Washington questions the sustainability of its transatlantic alliance with these countries: 'It is an open question whether they will view their place in the world, or their alliance with the United States, in the same way as those who signed the NATO charter.' The conclusion is that the US needs to help European nations get back on track, and the explicit aim is 'cultivating resistance to Europe's current trajectory within European nations'.[46]

What are we to make of this? 'It is a brazen declaration of intent for a regime change' – a political transformation forced by the US, like before in Cuba and Iraq, and now attempted in Venezuela and Iran – explains Catherine de Vries. 'For the United States, the foreign threat is no longer Russia or China, it is the European Union.'

Trump aims to bring about this change in Europe by forging a new 'alliance for civilization'. He is pledging his support and partnership to 'patriotic parties' that, just like him, reject the EU and the liberal values it represents. It was also in this context that he announced sanctions against former EU commissioner Thierry Breton and four other European citizens 'agents of the global censorship-industrial complex'[47] because of their work on digital sovereignty and preventing the online incitement of hate.[48] Make no mistake, de Vries says: 'The US administration is overtly working to reshape European democracies ideologically, by actively meddling in EU politics and domestic affairs: building and funding networks, publicly endorsing far-right parties, leveraging Europe's dependence on American Big Tech and now imposing targeted sanctions against individuals.'[49]

The Great Reset: an attack on the EU

Behind the scenes, cooperation between Trump and the far right in Europe goes much further: there is active work on a concrete plan to dismantle the European Union from within, driven by like-minded groups outside politics. The brains behind these efforts are three ultra-conservative foundations in the United States and Europe, namely the Heritage Foundation (US), Ordo

Iuris (Poland) and the Mathias Corvinus Collegium (Hungary), which all have direct connections with far-right politicians at home and abroad.

First, the Heritage Foundation – the conservative think tank behind Project 2025, a blueprint for dismantling American democracy that was just waiting for a far-right, conservative president: Donald J. Trump.[50] Its president, Kevin Roberts, is Trump's informal envoy to Europe, tasked with breathing life into the desired 'alliance for civilization'.[51]

Then there are those in Europe: Ordo Iuris, an ultraconservative Catholic lobby group known for its anti-LGBTQI+ and anti-abortion positions; and the Mathias Corvinus Collegium, a private education institution and influential Fidesz think tank rolled into one. In September 2024, these two joined forces with the Heritage Foundation to lay the groundwork for a plan to 'reform the EU',[52] following the example of Project 2025. Six months later, they produced a document titled 'The Great Reset'.

But wait, wasn't that the name of the Covid recovery plan for the global economy announced at the 2020 World Economic Forum? It was indeed. That plan soon became fodder for a widespread conspiracy theory with the same name by which right-wing extremists such as Trump's MAGA movement accused a global elite of having orchestrated the pandemic in order to impose a new, socialist world order – another echo of the stab-in-the-back myth.[53]

And now, 'The Great Reset' is the title of an actual proposal to dismantle the EU,[54] which is described by the authors as an 'authoritarian' and 'woke' 'Frankenstein's monster'.[55] Among other things, they want to get rid of the European Commission and the European Court of Justice, or even rebuild the EU from scratch on the basis of à-la-carte cooperation. Those behind the Great Reset initiative say they're in talks with parties across Europe.[56]

Compared with Project 2025, the result of decades of work, 'The Great Reset' reads like a sales brochure – in this case for the demolition of the EU. And for now, it doesn't look like the plan will actually be rolled out the same way Project 2025 was. But it does show that far-right parties can count on powerful international allies and accomplices who have no real interest in their domestic ultranationalist projects, yet will nonetheless help undermine the EU and the rules-based order. The reasoning they give dovetails perfectly with the fascist playbook: to save European nations from an evil left-wing elite that has institutionalized its rotten, progressive ideas in the EU – opening the gates for immigrants flooding the continent and destroying its civilization.

Genocide against Palestinians: a laboratory for global fascism

The genocide against Palestinians, which escalated following the Hamas attack on 7 October 2023, lies at the heart of the undermining of the international rules-based, legal order. It is both a catalyst for the agenda of the transnational pact of far-right leaders, ultraconservatives and corporate elites, and a tool to silence anyone defending that rules-based order. Israel's attempt to eradicate the Palestinian people is now considered one of the gravest violations of international law by a – nominally – democratic country since World War II.

It remains unchecked, as many European countries as well as the United States continue to back Israel's violence. Militarily, by continuing to supply and buy weapons. Diplomatically, by blocking sanctions, and then by forcing through – under the guise of a 'peace plan'[57] – what amounts to a business deal that aims to crush Palestinian identity, culture and sovereignty, herd the remaining Palestinian people into tightly controlled enclaves, and clear the coastline for profitable beach-front development.[58]

Palestine has effectively become a laboratory for future warfare and social control[59] – a testing ground for high-tech weaponry,[60] surveillance technology,[61] repression strategies, and the ultimate limits of international law. The lessons learned there are becoming human-tested tools and tactics for today's playbook of global fascism.

Officially, Israel's allies are acting under the pretext of Israel's 'right to self-defence' following the 7 October 2023 attack. But that right does not apply in this context. Israel is not defending itself against another country; it is itself the occupier.[62] As the International Court of Justice already ruled in 2004, Israel therefore has a duty to protect everyone in both Israel *and* occupied Palestine.[63]

What does apply, however, is the international law protecting citizens against genocide, war crimes and crimes against humanity.[64] Yet when it comes to Palestine, the silence is deafening. Because international law is ignored, 'the international rules-based, legal order is at serious risk' said Sigrid Kaag, the former UN special coordinator for the Middle East peace process, shortly before she stepped down in June 2025.[65] This raises questions. What on earth has possessed Western governments to so blatantly throw international law to the dogs? And where does all this end?

The answers to those questions do not lie in a lack of information about the situation in Gaza – in fact, there is an overabundance of evidence, and in early 2024 this led the International Court of Justice to find that there was a real risk of genocide.[66] The International Criminal Court in turn issued arrest warrants for Israel's prime minister, Benjamin Netanyahu, and his former defence minister, Yoav Gallant (plus three leaders of the military arm of Hamas who have since been killed).[67] Among scholars too, there is a broad consensus that what is happening in Gaza is a case of genocide.[68] In autumn 2025, even the UN Independent International Commission concluded flatly: 'genocide'.[69]

Nor did countries have to wait for international rulings to take action. What is more: under countless laws and treaties, UN member states are *obliged* to prevent genocide, even without conclusive legal rulings. Member states each have their own legislation on the matter. The Netherlands, for example, has laid down principles that the government and parliament can apply independently to establish (the risk of) genocide and take action accordingly.[70] As the Dutch parliament did in 2021, when it recognized crimes against the Yezidis by Islamic State (IS) as genocide.[71]

Nonetheless, Israel's allies continue to support it. This amounts to an unparalleled undermining of international law. Or, as Kaag put it, 'International humanitarian law has effectively been buried along with the thousands of children killed in Gaza and the hostages still held in captivity.'[72]

That law is far from perfect, but it matters. The International Criminal Tribunal for the former Yugoslavia brought 161 suspects to court for crimes such as the genocide in Srebrenica. American soldiers who tortured Iraqi prisoners in Abu Ghraib were convicted under international law. And when Vladimir Putin illegally invaded Ukraine, the European Union imposed sanctions on the Russian president. Violations of human rights, in short, have had diplomatic, legal and economic consequences. Or rather: until recently, war criminals at least tried to hide what they were doing.

But it is precisely that law and those standards that are now under pressure as Israel is being defended tooth and nail by its allies. Why? Because this is where the interests of far-right politicians and their (unwitting) allies and accomplices converge.

There are countless politicians who still believe that the founding of the state of Israel settled the moral debt for the Holocaust, and Israel therefore deserves their unquestioning support. Others simply do not dare speak out of fear of being labelled antisemitic. Then there are the ultraconservative Christians who see Israel as the promised land chosen by God for the Jews.[73] And of course, the banks, tech giants, arms dealers and security companies making a fortune off the genocide and Israel's occupation.[74]

All reasons for bending international law, but not necessarily to break it. It is a different matter for the far-right leaders who are on a strong march forward in Europe and the United States. They genuinely want to break international law. Ensuring that 'the legal order is at serious risk' is precisely the point.

Their support has just as much to do with their own political agendas as with Israel itself. In an opinion piece for the right-wing conservative news site Breitbart, Dutch far-right politician Geert Wilders explained why he supports Israel: 'Not just because it is the frontline against the totalitarian threat of Islam, not only because we support the Jewish homeland in their fight for existence, but also because it is a beacon for nations striving to maintain their national identity.'[75]

To put it bluntly: Israel is a model of the homogenous nation state that far-right politicians want, protected by borders that are 'strong and guarded' (Wilders's own words), and – following this line of reasoning – maintained through means such as occupation, walls, fences, totalitarian digital surveillance, kidnapping, ethnic cleansing – and, now, genocide.

Or to put it even more bluntly: mass atrocities to dispose of anyone who doesn't fit the image of the homogenous nation? Perfectly fine.

Critical voices are also being silenced at home

Gaza is no longer just a catalyst for the international agenda of the far right. It has become a tool to silence critics at home. Now that international law and the attendant institutions have been undermined, it is the turn of the people who defend them to become a target. Once again, the fascist playbook is at work: every fascist portrays independent critics as part of a plot by the so-called enemy, in this case Muslims.

There is even a concrete plan. Here the transnational network on which so many rising far-right politicians rely comes back into the picture. The blueprint for repressing anyone who speaks out against the genocide was concocted by the Heritage Foundation (yes, them again!), this time in the form of Project Esther.[76] Officially, the project's aim is to combat antisemitism, a real and growing threat in Western societies. But it reads like a strategy to muzzle political opponents.

The plan was drawn up by a task force predominantly made up of far-right and ultraconservative groups. Jewish organizations, as *The New York Times* revealed, were barely represented.[77] Moreover, the plan exclusively targets left-wing antisemitism; right-wing antisemitism isn't mentioned once. This despite the fact that antisemitism is rampant on the right: according to a survey by the conservative Manhattan Institute, a quarter of Republicans under fifty openly self-identify as anti-Jewish, and almost 40 per cent of all Republicans believe the Holocaust was exaggerated.[78]

Project Esther states that the global pro-Palestine movement is part of the anti-American 'Hamas Support Network', an entity invented by the drafters of the plan. Once again, a perverse inversion: anyone who protests genocide and stands up for international law is branded a terrorist, a threat to that very legal order. It is a framing that makes anyone who upholds and adheres to international law suspect: UN officials, aid workers, activists, academics, journalists, and even Jewish human rights organizations such as Jewish Voice for Peace.

The plan has since been implemented by Trump: students criticizing Israel have been arrested, international students' visas have been withdrawn, travellers to the US are being screened for alleged antisemitism, protestors' personal data is shared with immigration services, and universities are being hit with financial sanctions for alleged connections with the so-called Hamas Support Network.[79] Sanctions have been issued against UN special rapporteur for Palestine Francesca Albanese[80] and eleven ICC prosecutors and judges.[81]

Of course, casting suspicions this way is nothing new: Israel has been doing it for decades. Abroad, the country maintains and funds a network of influencers and NGOs that intimidate critics and report positively on Israel; in 2025 alone, an extra 137 million euros was allocated for this purpose.[82] The network spreads fake reports of alleged antisemitism at aid organizations and the UN.[83] It brands Palestinian journalists and aid workers as terrorists, then has their funding cut[84] – or even has them murdered in targeted killings.[85] Counterterrorism has thus become code for undermining international law, and targeting organizations and people protected under that law.

Israel's allies have long supported this. What's new, however, is that Israel's allies in the West – especially in countries where the far right is strong – are now adopting this logic wholesale to muzzle dissenting voices within their own borders.

Not only in the US with Project Esther, but in Europe too. And not only by the far right, but by centrist parties that, once again, are emerging as willing accomplices. In the UK, an overwhelming majority in the House of Commons declared Palestine Action – an activist group that has been trying to stop arms exports to Israel through disruptive and occasionally illegal action – a terrorist organization, despite urgent warnings from the UN[86] and human rights groups like Amnesty International.[87] The following day, protestors with placards who expressed support for Palestine Action – including lawyers, a professor emeritus and an eighty-three-year-old priest – were arrested under terrorism laws.[88] By the start of September 2025, the number of people arrested had already reached 900.[89] Even after the High Court ruled that the ban on the group was unlawful, it remained in place while the government prepared an appeal – leaving protesters in 'legal limbo'.[90]

The Netherlands is following suit. A bill is now in the making to criminalize 'publicly expressing support for terrorist organizations'.[91] The examples from the US and the UK show that, once such a law is in place, it is a small step towards criminalizing anti-genocide protests. The watermelon – the symbol for Palestine and anti-genocide protests – was already declared a sign of support for Hamas by the leader of the Dutch liberal party (VVD), Dilan Yeşilgöz, in September 2024.[92]

And what about the hundreds of thousands of Dutch people who, again and again, drew a red line against the Dutch government's support for Israel with the so-called Red Line protests? PVV leader Geert Wilders called it 'a pro-Hamas demo by confused people',[93] and he never misses an opportunity to point to 'the antisemitism and hatred for Jews amongst the extreme left and radical immigrants'.[94] Yet – and this says a lot – when his supporters later marched through The Hague like a far-right gang of thugs, chanting antisemitic slogans and waving Dutch National Socialist Movement (NSB) flags from the Nazi era, with some of them giving Hitler salutes: not a word.

Israel's methods of violence and expulsion against the Palestinians are being justified under the pretext of protecting the rights of the Jewish minority. Meanwhile, it is not getting any safer for Jewish people. Under the pretext of protecting a people from genocide, fascist methods are being normalized, says Naomi Klein, until 'even that flimsy façade is dropped in favour of a purer white nationalism with no need for Jewish cover'.[95]

Among parts of the MAGA movement, that facade is beginning to crumble.[96] In November 2025, political commentator Tucker Carlson gave right-extremist influencer Nick Fuentes a huge platform (in an interview Trump personally defended[97]) to spread antisemitic conspiracy theories, citing Israel's atrocities in Gaza as proof of the plot. 'For decades, antisemitism was a taboo; now, anyone who crosses the line feels untouchable and has already targeted other minorities before,' says Jewish American writer Elad Nehorai. The result is downright bizarre: 'This is how a genocide can be committed in the name of protecting Jews, while Jews are simultaneously attacked in the name of the genocide in Gaza.'[98]

Crony capitalism beats out ideology

The question then is: why are the advocates of international law being silenced? Why is this motley crew of far-right politicians and their global network of allies and accomplices so keen to quit international institutions? Is it really to fight antisemitism and muzzle 'liberal' views, or are other interests at play?

Of course, the network includes groups acting from deeply rooted convictions, such as ultraconservatives, tech-utopians, accelerationists, xenophobes, transphobes and Islamophobes. And there are fanatic right-extremist groups like White Lives Matter and the Proud Boys among the accomplices of modern-day fascism. Their role, however, is primarily that of 'useful idiots', explains former Dutch intelligence officer Jelle Postma. They instigate chaos and help mobilize voters emotionally to get far-right leaders elected. As a result, they offer cover for a strategy that essentially seeks to dismantle all countervailing power and dominate the global market.

To understand this, we have to go back to the origins of the international rules-based, legal order – built as it was on the rubble of World War II with cries of 'Never again!' 'If Europe is to be saved from infinite misery, and indeed from final doom,' Winston Churchill said in 1946, 'there must be this act of faith in the European family, this act of oblivion against all crimes and follies of the past.'[99] There was a shared realization that sustainable peace required far-reaching international cooperation based on values like freedom, equality, the rule of law and human rights. This understanding resulted in the Universal Declaration of Human Rights, which served as the foundation for a string of other treaties and institutions such as the United Nations and the European Union. It brought the West a long period of peace, security and economic prosperity.

But this legal order was not just idealistic. Above all, it was a way to restore Western domination. After the war, the debt of guilt towards the Jewish people was offloaded onto the Palestinians, who were driven off their land en masse to make room for a nation state for Holocaust survivors – outside Europe and conveniently out of sight of those who had allowed them to be subjected to untold suffering. Moreover, the rules-based order of the West and its promotion of liberal democracy worldwide was diametrically opposed to the communism of the Soviet Union and China – who, in turn, also sought to extend their sphere of influence across the world. The colonialism of the nineteenth and early twentieth centuries was replaced by new, but no less destructive, kinds of domination: economic, technological and ideological. Big business – from oil barons to tech giants – supported the development of the liberal international order in exchange for tax havens and a relatively free global market.

After the fall of the Berlin Wall in 1989, the liberal world order became the dominant one. Countries like Russia, China and Iran seemingly had to conform in a world that enforced liberal democracy and free markets as the norm. Those days are now over. As Anne Applebaum explains in *Autocracy Inc.* (2024), the pursuit of profit is now these countries' highest geopolitical priority. They spin a web of global interdependencies in the form of arms deals, energy contracts, surveillance systems, infrastructure, propaganda and diplomatic support. A new global order structured around the law of the jungle – naked power politics, geared towards increasing autocrats' wealth and smothering critical voices, both within and beyond international borders. To paraphrase Applebaum, it is no longer about ideals, but about deals.[100] It is against this geopolitical backdrop that the political shifts in the West are taking place.

What is striking is that these strategies are no longer confined to apparatchiks, ayatollahs and oligarchs in traditionally autocratic countries. Leaders like Trump using fascist strategies to hollow out democracy in their own countries are moving in this direction too. 'They see the state as a company in which they're the only shareholder,' explains Catherine de Vries.

The sums involved are astronomical. Journalist David D. Kirkpatrick has estimated that Trump and his family have made no less than $3.4 billion in profit since his first term in the White House.[101] And if the presidency becomes a personal revenue model, international treaties simply stand in the way. As de Vries concludes: 'It's hard to plunder state coffers if you have to respect international agreements.'

But it's also about economic power, stresses Jelle Postma. 'If, like Trump, you start a trade war to gain control of markets, it helps if you can also split large power blocks like the EU. Deals with twenty-seven fragmented countries are simply easier to force through than a single deal with one strong European Union.'

The billionaires who support far-right politicians are also doing the math. Companies across big tech, big oil, big pharma and big finance in the West are betting on the far right, and not only because they're running up against the limits of what they can do within the liberal world order, with all its treaties on sustainability and human rights and its rules against monopolies. In exchange for their support, they're also being handed mega-contracts[102] and insider knowledge on markets, along with privileged access to those markets.[103] It's no coincidence that the United States is going all in on the European Union watering down climate legislation and deregulating the tech sector,[104] while also framing European human rights policy as a blatant violation of those very same human rights.[105]

Here, then, is the answer to why the far right has launched its attack on the rules-based, legal order: money, power and impunity. Crony capitalism beats out ideological convictions. And so authoritarian leaders are steering the world towards a new, multipolar world order in which they can all go about their divine business unpunished.

The EU's defence lines

The European Union – bastion of liberal values and rule-of-law guarantees protecting its member states against authoritarianism – is an explicit target for both Trump and Putin, as well as the far-right parties in Europe drawing from the same fascist playbook. These parties are finding each other ever more readily in their efforts to weaken the EU. Aided by a temporary, opportunistic, transnational pact of allies and accomplices, they have even managed to inflict serious damage on the international liberal order. But their greater mission to dismantle the EU and remove a major obstacle to their power grab back home remains for now stuck in brochure-sized plans. There's a real chance it will stay that way. After all, Europe is not the US. Individual member states are not economic or military superpowers, and their governments must constantly strike a balance between national and European politics.

The European Union has strong constitutional guardrails to protect liberal democracy across the continent – guarantees against precisely the kind of behaviour these far-right politicians are now displaying.

How robust are these guardrails? I put that question to Hanneke van Eijken, professor of rule of law and democracy at Utrecht University. 'It is the very core: if you strip the entire European project back to its essence, then you end up at *peace*,' she replied. 'The European rule of law is a space where peace can grow because there is room for dialogue between people.'

These are more than just fine words. First, there is the so-called Article 7 procedure. Under this article, a member state that undermines European values can lose its voting rights in the European Council – the most powerful body in the EU, where heads of state and government take joint decisions. But there's a catch: the Council has to vote unanimously to strip a member state of those rights. 'And that makes it extremely difficult,' Van Eijken explained. 'Some member states cover each other's backs.' Case in point: Hungary. Since 2018, the European Parliament has been calling in vain for an Article 7 procedure – *seven years* later, the Council has yet to vote on it.[106]

Then there is the second line of defence: the Court of Justice of the European Union. It can hold member states to their constitutional obligations. 'The Court can bite,' Van Eijken told me. 'But it needs to bite more and more often. Heads of government ignore the very treaties they themselves signed, and then it falls to the Court to hold them to account. Then they blame the judges for the consequences of the political decisions they themselves took. The Court is thus deliberately turned into a punching bag.'

Efforts to undermine the European Court of Human Rights are perhaps the most worrying. This court allows individuals, groups, organizations and even countries to file complaints against members of the Council of Europe* under the European Convention on Human

---

* The continent's leading human rights institution, which includes non-EU-members as well – not to be confused with the European Council.

Rights.[107] Among other things, this treaty prohibits discrimination and guarantees the right to asylum. It is the last line of defence for minority rights.

That is precisely why it is telling that, in May 2025, nine countries where the far right is firmly entrenched – including Italy, Austria, Poland and Belgium – jointly sent an open letter of complaint about the Court of Human Rights. Their objection: that the judges restrict their national room for manoeuvre by holding them to European fundamental rights.[108] A textbook example of the far-right framing of independent judges as an obstacle to 'the will of the people'.

The European Union's defence mechanisms are robust, but only if member states respect them. And that's where things often go wrong. The issue starts with the political parties' actions at the national level. That's where, with few exceptions, right-wing conservative parties are ever more ready to adopt far-right positions, propagate them within the EU and govern alongside far-right parties – a key explanation for the far right's recent rise and growing influence in the EU.

One well-known example of this dynamic is the Netherlands. In 2023, when the liberal VVD adopted the far-right PVV's migration agenda and no longer ruled out governing with the PVV, Geert Wilders's party scored a historic election victory, topping the polls. During the year that followed, Wilders succeeded in firmly establishing his extremist ideas at the heart of national politics. His rise shows how quickly the far right can become normalized.

4. A case study: the fascist playbook in the Netherlands

What about Dutch politics? After the United States and Europe, has fascism now breached the Dutch polder?

The general feeling in the Netherlands is that this is an overstatement. Yes, in recent years a long line of far-right populists have tried to push the limits of liberal democracy in The Hague, but their programmes met with strong resistance from both voters and moderate parties. A real breakthrough seemed far off.

The far right ultimately has little chance of fundamentally undermining democracy and the rule of law – or so the thinking goes. We're talking about the Netherlands after all, that wholesome, decent country that practically invented the art of compromise – where it's not the done thing to stand out.

What is more, critics on the far right will say, if there has been any hostility and violence, it has been directed at the far right. In the 1980s, for example, leader of the extreme-right Centre Democrats (CD) party Hans Janmaat – convicted for anti-immigrant statements like 'full means full' and 'our own people first' – was the target of an anti-fascist attack. In 2002, LPF leader Pim Fortuyn – who wanted to scrap the constitutional ban on discrimination[1] – was murdered by left-wing extremist Volkert van der Graaf. And Islam critic and conservative-liberal VVD politician Ayaan Hirsi Ali moved to the US after receiving death threats and getting dragged into a prolonged conflict with fellow party member Rita Verdonk, who questioned her Dutch citizenship. Far-right Forum for Democracy founder Thierry Baudet – who talked about the 'homeopathetic dilution' of 'boreal Europe' (meaning Aryan or white, and with strong echoes of the Nazi belief in a lost Nordic world) – was hit on the head twice, first with an umbrella, then a beer bottle. And then there's far-right PVV leader Geert Wilders. He has received so many threats for his Islamophobic opinions that he has lived under protection for twenty years.

Across the world, however, the Netherlands is also seen as a textbook example of how the far right can be normalized – a crucial requirement for fascist strategies to succeed.[2] The 2023 parliamentary elections fit perfectly with Robert Paxton's theory that moderate politicians pave the way for fascist leaders by legitimizing their positions.

The big name here is Wilders, the sole member and authoritarian leader of the far-right Party for Freedom,[3] which joined the Patriots for Europe in the European Parliament in 2024. Guest of honour and keynote speaker at CPAC in Hungary that same year, Wilders has been at the heart of political controversy for decades. So familiar is he that his downright inflammatory, hate-mongering statements now sound like a dripping tap. Annoying, but not annoying enough to get out of bed for. A sound that has become part of the house.

Over time, however, his party has grown in influence through the actions of centre-right politicians who adopted and normalized its positions. This is especially due to the ideological acrobatics of former liberal VVD prime minister Mark Rutte, who once said that in politics you have to dance with 'whoever is on the dance floor'.[4] Even, apparently, if they're called Trump, Orbán or Erdoğan, and they are trying to demolish the foundations on which that dance floor is built. That's how 'Teflon Mark' danced his party to the right.[5] He was willing to overlook Wilders's most controversial ideas to get support for his minority government. And though he then closed the door to further cooperation, he nonetheless adopted several of Wilders's extreme positions on migration and asylum, and as a result helped to normalize them.[6]

Rutte's successor Dilan Yeşilgöz reopened the door to Wilders in 2023. Three years previously, Wilders had been convicted for group insult after leading crowds in chanting 'fewer, fewer, fewer Moroccans'. Thanks to the VVD, he won the 2023 elections in a landslide with exactly the same rhetoric. In the space of one election campaign, what was once unthinkable had become normal.[7]

Fascism in the polder

Wilders himself was normalized too, promptly rebranded by some media as Geert *Milders* – the man whose sharp edges had been polished away as soon as power came within reach. This is when the common Dutch conviction that 'the soup is never eaten as hot as it's served' became a problem.

For years, Wilders had followed a clear strategy of intimidation, polarization and dehumanization in order to mobilize white Dutch people against a supposed Islamic enemy. He weaponized the language of law and order to settle scores with 'mass immigration', 'woke multiculturalism', politically motivated progressive judges, 'scumbag' journalists, the 'radical-left church', Muslims, and whichever minority group came next.

Some academics have a name for this: polder fascism.[8] It sprouts from the drained and reclaimed soil and creeps through the cracks of the Dutch culture of consensus and compromise. Fed not only by Wilders, but also by other parties that draw from the same playbook: Forum for Democracy (FvD), for example, whose leader claims the Netherlands is a 'sham democracy' and that the only one standing up to it is Russian president Vladimir Putin.[9] Then there's the rural populism of the Farmer–Citizen Movement (BBB) – city–countryside divide, check! – adding a generous shovel of artificial fertilizer to polder fascism.

Wilders topped the polls, and the PVV joined the Schoof coalition government in 2024 as its largest party, together with the liberal VVD, the conservative NSC and the far-right BBB. In less than a year, under the cover of a decent political compromise – he turned down the role of prime minister, claiming his 'love for the country and voters' was greater than that for his own position[10] – Wilders managed to force his extreme ideas on the centre parties and erode long-standing democratic norms.

That year, there was barely any opposition. Not from the cabinet headed by a bland, politically inexperienced prime minister who could not withstand the pressure

Wilders put on him via X. Nor from the coalition party leaders, whose limited understanding of the game plan for liberal democracy trapped them in short-term tactics.

Meanwhile, in a classic fascist reflex, the PVV Speaker of the House Martin Bosma intervened in the language used in the Dutch parliament. When proposed measures were appropriately described as 'extreme right', he disapproved of the term. In his view, it implied a comparison with Nazis and was therefore inappropriate for parliamentary debate. The opposition was thus stripped of the language it needed to name what it was fighting. And so the government continued to inch towards Wilders's agenda.

So are these recent developments 'polder fascism'? When I put this to fascism scholar Finchelstein, he immediately replied, 'Geert Wilders is a typical wannabe fascist. What is happening in the Netherlands is part of a global phenomenon in which populism is turning into fascism.'[11] And when we compare it with Jason Stanley's ten instruments of fascism, the signs are everywhere.

How Geert Wilders uses the ten instruments of fascism

Like the fascists of old, Wilders is employing the ten instruments of fascism. He, too, subjects the country to a myth: that the Netherlands was once proud, safe and 'ours' – but has been ruined by mass immigration, a hatred of farmers, and the climate dictates of unelected European commissioners. The PVV's 2023 campaign slogan, 'Put the Dutch first again', promised a return to a time of closed borders, farmers free to farm, streets devoid of mosques, and ordinary Dutch people with names like Geert or Marjolein (*not* Mohammed or Fatima). Because, as the 2025 slogan declared, 'This land is yours'.

Wilders, too, poisons the debate with lies about 'criminal migrants' and 'sham refugees'. He has wrongly claimed that half of all babies born in big cities in the Netherlands are of non-Western backgrounds, that a third of the population on the African continent wants to 'flood' Europe as a 'tsunami' of migrants, and that some municipalities hand asylum seekers credit cards with free money.[12] Without intervention, he says, the Netherlands would transform into an Islamist caliphate by 2050.[13] That's why he wants not only a complete halt to asylum applications, but also far-reaching measures to strip certain people of their passports or residence permits – for example after a criminal conviction, or by banning dual nationality, which would cost all Dutch Moroccans their Dutch passports. Of Dutch people with a migration background 'who don't integrate', he demands that they 'remigrate': a one-way ticket to their country of origin or that of their ancestors, in exchange for giving up their Dutch passport.[14]

Wilders, too, intimidates independent thinkers. He has called journalists 'scumbags' and 'creepy left-wing activists',[15] and gave his spokesman strict instructions to 'fend off and manage' the press.[16] He communicates primarily via X, his preferred propaganda platform, where his 1.6 million followers make him by far the most followed Dutch politician.[17] Meanwhile, the cabinet in which the PVV was the largest party made drastic cuts to art, culture and public broadcasting – which, according to Wilders, 'primarily produces propaganda'.[18] If it were up to him, not a single cent would go to the Dutch public broadcaster, the NPO, and its studios would be torn down to make room for apartment blocks.[19]

Wilders, too, has tried to implant 'Great Replacement' conspiracy theories in the public consciousness. He says it is happening through an 'Islamic invasion of testosterone bombs with beards', who are coming for our 'houses, benefits and women'.[20] Referring to the death threats he has received, he has said: 'If we don't stop Islamization, then my fate will become yours. And your children's.'[21] It all amounts to 'national suicide', he claims.[22] Wilders says the 'radical-left church', i.e. the Green/Labour party GroenLinks-PvdA (now Progressief Nederland), is part of the conspiracy. With imagery worthy of 1930s Nazi propaganda, a Wilders campaign ad suggested that a vote for GroenLinks-PvdA was a vote for a threatening older woman wearing a headscarf. The depicted alternative was a friendly young PVV blonde. The slogan under the image: 'It's your choice.'[23] Wilders repeats these conspiracy theories until people choose to believe him. This way, he creates a new political reality that sucks in parties from all sides.[24]

Wilders, too, believes that the institutions in the international rules-based order are turning against the Netherlands' interests. He would gladly do away with the International Criminal Court,[25] calls the European Union a 'dictatorship'[26] and dismisses development cooperation as a 'left-wing hobby'.[27] He turned off the 'money tap for gender equality'[28] as soon as he had the chance,[29] and he wants to withdraw from the UN Refugee Convention, the European Convention on Human Rights, the European

Convention on Nationality, and other treaties he claims are impeding the Netherlands.[30]

Wilders, too, calls for a clear hierarchy in society, with those who are white and 'true' Dutchmen at the top. He claims they are being 'disadvantaged and discriminated against' under the pretext of 'positive discrimination'. Wilders wants this 'ethnic cleansing' to stop. He wants to fire the Dutch National Coordinator against Discrimination and Racism ASAP, and bring back the racist Dutch holiday tradition of blackface known as Black Pete. For Wilders, it's an existential matter: 'If [we] defend your identity... we ensure our survival.'[31]

Wilders, too, propagates rigid views on gender, claiming that the 'woke dictatorship' is indoctrinating children with gender ideology. His 2025 election programme declared: 'For the PVV there are only two sexes: man and woman... we will stop woke policies and scrap gender propaganda in schools.'[32] Not only does he want to ban trans women from women's sports, prisons, toilets and changing rooms, he demands an end to the 'left-liberal sexual indoctrination through education'.

Wilders, too, idealizes the countryside, where hard-working farmers – 'the heart of the Netherlands'[33] – are being crushed by 'left-liberal madmen'[34] from the big cities and their 'environmental hobbies': 'Their [farming] land will be used to build new centres for asylum seekers. Madness.'[35] He portrays white Dutch people as hard-working victims of the corrupt, lazy Amsterdam chattering classes.[36]

Finally, Wilders, too, weaponizes law and order. He has called the Dutch parliament 'fake', wants to abolish the Dutch Senate (which forces Dutch politics towards compromise),[37] accused 'stark-raving mad judges' of interfering in politics, and threatened to take civil servants and public prosecutors to court.[38] He also wants to introduce laws that will erode fundamental rights, such as withdrawing voting rights from dual nationals, discriminating against migrants with residence permits, using terrorism laws to withdraw passports, and taking alleged 'jihad sympathizers' into administrative detention without a court order.

Once the Schoof cabinet – where the PVV was the biggest coalition partner, though Wilders didn't take a ministerial role in it himself – took up office in 2024, Wilders opted for confrontation. He wanted to declare a state of emergency to 'save' the Netherlands from the 'plague of asylum seekers' and a 'tsunami of criminal migrants'. This would grant the government far-reaching (temporary) powers, sidelining parliament and existing laws.

Attempting to declare a state of emergency without due cause – like a war or a global health crisis – is yet another major indication that Wilders is following the fascist playbook. It is a way of diminishing the checks on power that are a feature of a liberal democracy. It also echoes Hitler, who used the so-called Enabling Act of 1933 to seize absolute power. Or Orbán, who rewrote Hungary's constitution in 2011 to do the same.[39] Or Trump, who used executive orders and ancient war laws to bypass Congress.

When coalition partner New Social Contract (NSC) blocked this power grab, Wilders triggered a succession of government crises. They revolved around asylum laws, the 'polarizing conduct' of PVV ministers, and military support for Ukraine.[40] These crises produced no solutions, but rather strained the coalition and strengthened Wilders's position.[41]

In the end, this led to the collapse of the Schoof cabinet on 3 June 2025, after only eleven months in office. A collapse that showed that more had been destroyed than just a coalition, as the PVV had been going down in the polls for months. In the run-up to the elections that followed, Wilders reached for yet another classic fascist tactic: the Big Lie.

Geert Wilders's Big Lie

Russian American journalist M. Gessen aptly describes this type of lie as the 'bully lie': 'It is the lie of the bigger kid who took your hat and is wearing it – while denying that he took it. There is no defence against this lie because the point of the lie is to assert power.'[42]

This type of lie confronts citizens and politicians with a fundamental choice: remain faithful to the facts, or accept an alternative reality that is demonstrably false. Whoever opts for the latter abandons the very foundation of liberal democracy, a public debate based on facts.

Wilders's Big Lie was that his coalition partners wanted to turn 'the country into one big centre for asylum seekers'. This betrayed their agreement to draft 'the toughest asylum policy ever', he claimed, and would mean 'the ruin of the Netherlands'.[43] His demand: the signatures of the coalition party leaders on a list of additional asylum measures. He presented his lie as a sketchy ten-point plan during a tightly staged propaganda show disguised as a 'press conference'.

It was demonstrably untrue that the Netherlands was being turned into 'one big asylum centre' – a claim built on misrepresented statistics[44] – never mind facing ruin as a country. Equally important: his assertion that the other parties did not want the same tough asylum policy was also false. The coalition party leaders – who, like Wilders, were not part of the cabinet, but rather members of parliament without executive powers – said they *did* back his proposals and were even prepared to submit a joint motion on the matter. They 'still had a few questions' about implementation, but that was a matter for the cabinet.[45] Nothing was preventing the Minister for Asylum and Migration from getting to work. The fact that Wilders's plan violated international treaties, European legislation and possibly also the Dutch constitution wasn't even on the table.[46]

And, more importantly, who was the minister responsible for asylum policy? *None other than the PVV's very own Marjolein Faber*. The same minister who blocked a trip for asylum-seeking children to the Efteling theme park, refused royal honours for volunteers at the Central Agency for the Reception of Asylum Seekers (COA), and raised her profile with symbolic border controls and blatantly unfeasible emergency decrees (which the Dutch Council of State ruled to be 'negligent', 'ineffective' and 'legally problematic').[47]

The solution to the Netherlands supposedly being turned into an asylum centre thus lay in the hands of Wilders's own minister. No signature was needed from any party leader whatsoever. Nonetheless, Wilders walked his party out of the government. 'I had no choice,' he said. He immediately received messages of support from the White House[48] and his far-right friends across Europe.[49]

Of course he'd had a choice. But this was a strategic move to deploy the well-known fascist strategy, right at the heart of Dutch politics. Wilders, the saviour sent by the people, had been betrayed by a hypocritical elite bent on ruining the Netherlands by letting in an endless wave of asylum seekers. It was a lie that echoed the old stab-in-the-back myth and the conspiracies that followed.

So-called existential threat: check. Conspiracy by domestic elites: check. It was the polder variation on the Big Lie, designed to impose an alternative reality in which politicians and citizens alike were forced to choose: the facts, or an alternative world where extremism was the norm, undermining liberal democracy was a necessity for survival, and any politician who thought otherwise was a 'traitor to the nation'.

The centre–right wasn't being strategic, it was complicit

After Wilders's 'press conference', his coalition partners made a fatal misstep. Instead of standing firm on the principles of the rule of law, they defended themselves only against the lie that they were traitors. Faced with that accusation, they suddenly accepted Wilders's positions – until recently considered extreme – as serious options. Deploy the army against asylum seekers? No problem. Throw granted asylum seekers in asylum centres onto the street? Why not. Strip Dutch citizens with a migration background of their passports? Let's discuss it.

The coalition partners did point to the applicable democratic processes under which they could support Wilders's proposals, but about the fundamentally problematic substance of those proposals – the violation of treaties, the clash with the constitution – they said nothing. Some political commentators called this a tactic: the coalition partners never really wanted to implement Wilders's plans; they were just letting him fall on his own sword of political recklessness.

But here is what actually happened. When Wilders left the coalition, they copied his strategy. 'Treason,' said BBB minister Mona Keijzer. 'Ego,' said VVD leader Dilan Yeşilgöz. 'Totally irresponsible,' declared prime minister Dick Schoof. They all scrambled to stick the 'traitor' label Wilders had plastered on them right back onto Wilders himself. None of them denied migration was an existential threat, nor that there had been a betrayal. The debate focused solely on *who* was the traitor in this tragedy.

So there they were, squabbling over who had stolen whose proverbial hat. They had stooped to Wilders's playground tactics, instead of focusing on what was really at stake. Political parties have a fundamental duty to all voters that outweighs any partisan wrangling: to protect democracy and the rule of law. It should have been *them* who pulled the plug on the cabinet out of sheer astonishment and dismay at such unconstitutional proposals – not Wilders.

But that's not how it went. A year earlier, the coalition partners had needed Wilders to agree to a 'baseline to safeguard the constitution' before they would form a government with him.[50] When the cabinet fell, however, they were the ones shouting loudest – and they wanted exactly the same extremist policies as Wilders himself. Now it would be hard for them to back down. These were not smart political tactics; they prepared the way for the rise of polder fascism.

The Big Lie left its mark

Late in the evening on 3 July 2025, less than a month after the fall of the cabinet and following days of political chaos, the remaining coalition partners adopted the PVV proposal to criminalize irregular stays in the Netherlands. As a result, tens of thousands of people without valid papers[51] – along with anyone offering them care, food or accommodation – were declared fair game.[52]

That same evening, the parliament also adopted the Housing Act – hastily toughened at the PVV's insistence, just like the Asylum Act. The amendment effectively barred asylum seekers with permission to stay from being granted urgent status when applying for social housing. In other words: if you were born in the Netherlands and ended up on the street with your children, you got priority for social housing. But if your family held a residence permit – giving you the same rights and duties as any Dutch national – and you became homeless, you went to the bottom of the waiting list.[53] This amendment thus turned these families into second-class citizens, a violation of Article 1 of the Dutch constitution.[54]

Even the National Social Contract – the conservative party founded in 2023 to restore good governance and the rule of law, which had promised never to approve unconstitutional legislation and held the key to blocking these proposals – voted in favour.

One voice cut through that night: Esther Ouwehand, leader of the progressive Party for the Animals. She kept it brief. 'It is *un-be-liev-able* how quickly scapegoat policies have become the norm, and now even made law. This chamber is full of rabble-rousers. And full of people too cowardly to stand up to them.'[55]

Wilders, however, was in a festive mood. The next day, he treated 'PVV fans' to a trip to the Efteling,[56] the same theme park outing his minister had blocked for a group of child asylum seekers two months previously.

What do Wilders's supporters think?

A bully lie, explains M. Gessen, can cleave a society in two: those who are prepared to live in the alternative reality and those who resist it. And that brings us to the next group that needed to make up their mind about the fall of the government: the PVV's base.

For months after his 'press conference', Wilders kept repeating his lie. On 18 September 2025, during the General Financial Debate on the Budget Memorandum where the new government presented its new plans, Wilders asked a rhetorical question: 'Are we going to hand our country over to Africans, Arabs and criminal immigrants once and for all, or are we going to take back control? Are we going to choose to sink further into the quagmire of liberal left-wing multiculturalism or are we going to finally fight back?'[57]

The following weekend, right-wing extremist supporters of the PVV and other far-right parties decided to 'fight back' in their own way. They marched through the centre of The Hague like a band of thugs, smashing the windows of the progressive-liberal D66 party building, setting fire to a police car, attacking and injuring journalists and trying to force their way into empty government offices in the Binnenhof. They chanted antisemitic slogans, and some even made Nazi salutes. 'ASYLUM CENTRES = WAR', one placard declared.

The Dutch intelligence services pointed out that these supporters see violence as necessary to forestall a supposed 'race war' and establish a white ethnostate purged of 'woke ideology' and liberalism. They also noted that the far right's scapegoat policies in parliament have normalized and legitimized this violence – even as the parties officially reject it, as Wilders did during the riots in The Hague.[58]

Wilders's response to this assessment was telling. He rejected any and all responsibility, while rhetorically aligning himself with the agenda of the perpetrators, thereby legitimizing their motives in the same breath: 'People are angry... People are outraged... They just want their country back... And yes, I'm angry about that. Every time I think about the people you've all abandoned. Are you surprised that people are angry? ... They are outraged!'[59]

The vast majority of far-right supporters, however, are not violent extremists. Many have voted for the PVV and similar parties because they see immigration as an urgent problem. And that feeling is not pulled from thin air. The reception system for asylum seekers is indeed straining at the seams. But years of scapegoat politics has shifted the debate. It's no longer about how the system works, but rather about who does or does not belong in the Netherlands.

This narrative has grown roots. More than one-third of Dutch people now believe that 'Muslims and Muslim organizations' are trying to replace Europe's 'native population'.[60] The percentage is significantly higher among far-right supporters: four in ten PVV voters and as many as three-quarters of FvD voters.[61] The classic 'Great Replacement' theory has become mainstream. The result is a migration debate that barely touches the problems in the asylum system, and is dominated instead by chest-thumping rhetoric – close the borders, withdraw passports, restrict voting rights. Proposals that are in direct conflict with liberal democracy. Anyone who questions such ideas is no longer seen as a political opponent, but rather – to quote Wilders – as complicit in 'national suicide'.

And so suspicion of the democratic system itself has grown. One in three Dutch people fundamentally mistrusts the democratic order and sees the government as a 'robber state' – 'a company that sees citizens as part of its profit model'.[62] Research by Matthijs Rooduijn, professor of transdisciplinary social science at the University of Amsterdam, shows that only one in five PVV voters is satisfied with how liberal democracy works. In fact, many hold views diametrically opposed to it: more than half favour an authoritarian leader who bends the law now and then; less than half are bothered if that leader ignores parliament; and only 35 per cent fully support universal suffrage.[63] 'This alone is a worrying sign,' says Rooduijn. 'But even more worrying is that our liberal democracy itself is becoming part of the political struggle more and more often. Just like the environment, migration and Europe, it has now become part of a deeply polarized culture war.'[64]

And so the political playing field itself becomes the ball in a new political game, with PVV supporters in the stands cheering every goal Wilders scores against the team of democracy and the rule of law.

The far right on the rise

Wilders took a huge gamble in the summer of 2025 when he brought down the government over asylum policy. And he was punished for it. His party lost twelve of their thirty-seven seats in the elections that followed.[65] However, the difference with the progressive-liberal D66, who ultimately won, was only 29,668 votes.

There was no chance Wilders would immediately return to government following the 2025 elections: several centre-right parties had ruled out further cooperation with the PVV. Yet since Yeşilgöz's strategic blunder of leaving the door open to Wilders in 2023, he has shown that he can still become the biggest party. His exclusion feeds into a familiar narrative: Wilders, the voice of the people and saviour of the nation, is being thwarted by the allegedly anti-democratic establishment.[66] Like Trump or Orbán after their first terms, Wilders can sit in the opposition and keep hammering the victimhood story that he sacrificed his chance to become prime minister in 2023, only to be sidelined against the voters' wishes.

And that is what Wilders did – as soon as he lost the elections. He suggested that ballot boxes and voting software might have been rigged in several constituencies, implying that D66 and the ANP press agency, which he mockingly called the ANP66, were responsible. Less than a week later, Wilders declared himself the actual winner on X regardless, because he had received more preferential votes than D66 leader Rob Jetten. Four months later, he went further still, blaming the EU for his loss to the 'pro-EU, left-liberal D66': 'Perhaps had there been no EU interference, the PVV could have won the elections and I could have become prime minister instead of the wokeist Europeanist the Netherlands will now have.'[67]

This approach echoed that of Donald Trump after his 2020 election defeat: when you lose an election, sow doubt about the results before all the votes have been counted, and thus feed into the unfounded idea that it wasn't the voters who eliminated you but rather a plot by the established order. Or, if you ask Wilders, a plot by D66, the EU and, of course, the press.

Questioning election results is another move from the fascist playbook – characteristic of this modern variant, explains Federico Finchelstein. 'A classic populist would never even consider doing this. They need elections to be free and fair. But that is changing. Trump did it, Bolsonaro did it and now Wilders did it. Undermining the legitimacy of elections is how they reconnect to historic fascism.'[68]

The vast majority of Dutch voters naturally see through Geert Wilders's bizarre claims. The Dutch have an above-average level of trust in the integrity of elections. Around half of PVV voters have much less faith in elections, however, according to research from the Electoral Council.[69] And that's precisely the group Wilders is targeting, throwing them the red meat of his baseless claims. Conspiracy theorists will take care of the rest.

And they're moving fast, confirms former Dutch intelligence officer Jelle Postma, who has studied how trust in democracy was undermined online in the run-up to the

2025 Dutch elections. 'We're seeing a huge amount of disinformation about alleged election fraud in extreme-right groups online. These posts are not aimed at finding the truth, but rather at eroding trust in institutions. People start to doubt, and attention shifts from the election results to the conspiracy theory.'[70]

Despite his rhetoric, Wilders accepted the election results – just as Trump, despite everything, eventually peacefully transferred the presidency to his successor. 'The only reason these leaders ultimately accept the election results is that our democratic norms and guardrails are stronger today than they were before,' Finchelstein explains.[71]

Meanwhile, Wilders keeps the popular fury alive. Combined with support for other far-right parties, this could win him enough votes at the next election to form a far-right cabinet he could lead. And he would lead it the same way he leads his party: without contradiction.

The Netherlands is at a turning point

Once again, we have to ask: is this fascism? Not if you only compare it with the most extreme examples from the past. And even compared to Donald Trump, Geert Wilders pales. He has not organized a military parade for his birthday, been accused of storming the Capitol or had masked officers in plain clothes drag people off the streets.

But as historian Robert Paxton reminds us: 'We need not look for exact replicas, in which fascist veterans dust off their swastikas.' Quite the contrary: 'It is by understanding how past fascisms worked… that we may be able to recognize it.'[72]

Despite what many people in the Netherlands think – 'It can't happen here' – a clear shift is happening. And it fits a global trend in which classic populism is turning into a new kind of fascism. Wilders is an influential politician who is gradually undermining the foundations of our political freedoms and operating at the edges of liberal democracy– and sometimes beyond.[73] By drawing on strategies straight from the fascist playbook, he is showing more and more of his extreme-right tendencies.

Can fascism actually break through in the Netherlands? The country is at a turning point; Wilders has paved the way for extremism. Even though the PVV lost seats in the last elections, the far right as a whole grew. Together, far-right parties now hold almost one-third of all seats in the Dutch parliament. One of the parties that benefitted was the extreme-right FvD, whose co-leader Thierry Baudet once claimed the world is being ruled by 'evil reptiles'[74] and insists there is 'an existential threat' coming from 'those who are supposed to protect us', 'smuggling malicious, aggressive elements into our social body in unprecedented numbers'.[75] Several of its candidates standing in the 2026 local elections have openly expressed Nazi sympathies, yet remain fully backed by the party leadership.[76] Indeed, says Thomas Weber, professor of history and international affairs and leading scholar of Nazi Germany: 'FvD strongly echoes ideas of the Nazi party of the 1920s and comes eerily close to being its modern face.'[77] The rise of FvD at the PVV's expense is a telling example of how the boundaries of the acceptable are being pushed ever further into the extreme in Dutch politics.

But just as important as the rise and radicalization of the far right is the way moderate parties respond to it. As Paxton warned, fascism can quickly rear its ugly head when conservatives and right-wing liberals – in times of crisis and political stagnation – adopt the same language, ideas and tactics as the far right in the hope they'll hang on to voters.

The Dutch polder has proved to be fertile ground for precisely this behaviour. On 19 September 2025, a majority in the Dutch parliament voted to list Antifa as a terrorist organization. The fact that it was not their place to do so didn't seem to matter. Nor did the fact that Antifa isn't even an organization. It should worry us that a parliamentary majority regard a broad range of activists who oppose fascism as the enemy.

What is alarming is not only Wilders's now-threadbare hate-filled rhetoric, but how the moderate parties respond. The question is how far others are prepared to go along with him.

The answer, as we have seen, is: extremely far.

PART 3

Building a dam against fascism

Our power lies in the courage to take risks. The only way that you can stop something that is coming at full velocity is to throw yourself in front of it and try to block it. That wave of violence is gonna hit you – physically, emotionally, mentally.

You have to be ready to take the hit.

– Mariam Barghouti, Palestinian journalist,
De Correspondent (2025)

5. Together against fascism

Fascism destroys democracy from within. It starts with talk, not tanks. Elections, not a coup. And it takes hold thanks to people who think it won't happen here.

We're heading down that road again. Not with hundreds of thousands marching through the streets as they did in the twentieth century, but with the rise of far-right politicians in the US and Europe. With the quiet footsteps of lobbyists in the halls of power. With road maps from ultraconservative think tanks, armies of online trolls, Wokebusters and a Global Coalition Against Globalism. With the algorithms and billions of tech giants who control our digital public lives. And with the millions of people now walking along to the beat of the scapegoat drum.

Unlike in the twentieth century, when it was fuelled by a deep frustration at the outcome of World War I, today fascism is propelled by the existential threats of our time: climate change, disappearing biodiversity, extreme inequality, the threat of war, and a technological revolution replacing daily human interactions with apps and chatbots.

That's why Canadian authors Naomi Klein and Astra Taylor call it 'end times fascism': a fascism based on the idea that the world is on the brink of collapse. 'The governing ideology of the far right in our age of escalating disasters has become a monstrous, supremacist survivalism,' they say.[1] In this worldview, survival – which includes the maintenance of exorbitant lifestyles and the plundering of the planet it requires – is reserved for a privileged white, Christian minority entrenching itself behind ever-higher walls. Democracies transformed into heavily armed bunkers.

The far right's obsession with the nation state dovetails seamlessly with this worldview. This far-right ideal draws a cultural border between who, in their eyes, may live comfortably and who should be left by the wayside. In other words, those they regard worthy of human dignity and those they do not – the classic fascist hierarchy. Real solutions for complex problems then become unnecessary. What remains, say Klein and Taylor, is a cruel political project driven by a nostalgia for a past that never existed, and fuelled by the exclusion, humiliation and control of ever-growing numbers of people driven from an ever-shrinking scrap of liveable earth.

Paradoxically, these ultranationalist movements are united in a mission that crosses borders. They undermine not only national democracies, but also the international rules-based order. Turkish journalist Ece Temelkuran captures the transnational and high-tech nature of modern-day fascism with the term 'cloud fascism' – it is a dark cloud that is omnipresent, yet elusive.

Cloud fascism manifests itself digitally on the platforms of tech giants, to whom we are largely dependent for the exchange of information and ideas. And it manifests itself in the manhunts for migrants, the curtailing of trans rights, and support for the genocide of the Palestinian people. 'Cloud fascism is travelling the planet, showering us with acid rain,' writes Temelkuran. 'Yet each time it appears in a country, the citizens of the land behave as if it is the first time and only happening to them. The repeating astonishment marks the beginning of our retreat.'[2]

But we don't have to continue down this path. History not only tells us how fascism can advance, it also shows us that it can be stopped. By people who stand up for each other. By people who choose facts over fiction, connection over division, and humanity over dehumanization.

By people who understand: this is fascism.

Building a dam against fascism

Now that we know which forces we're dealing with, we are more resilient than we think. It begins with one clear principle: never 'obey in advance' leaders who want to curtail our freedoms.[3] It sounds obvious, but it is anything but. As Timothy Snyder explains at the start of his book *On Tyranny*, 'Most of the power of authoritarianism is freely given.' People may surrender their power for opportunistic or pragmatic reasons, or out of fear. Snyder calls it 'a political tragedy', because it is exactly this behaviour that paves the way for authoritarian powers.

Perhaps it happens when the asylum accommodation facility next door has been daubed with racist slogans and neighbours give it a wide berth instead of helping with the clean-up. When athletes laugh along with racist jokes in the locker room because they don't want to rock the boat. When Europeans scrub their timelines clean to keep their US visa options open. When CEOs ditch diversity policies because American clients are at stake.[4] When primary-school head teachers scrap sex education to appease conservative parents.[5] When public broadcasters censor criticism of Trump out of fear they'll be litigated into oblivion.[6] When writers decide not to publish because they're flooded with death threats.[7] When university rectors abolish certain academic positions in the hopes of retaining government funding. When researchers cut any mention of 'gender', 'inclusion' and 'climate' from grant proposals, to have a better chance of getting funding.[8] When festival organizers ban artists from making political statements on stage, to avoid a fuss.[9]

This is how it begins. This is what Snyder warns against.

'Stop!' he urges. 'This shows those in power how far they can go.'

The opposite is needed: we must fearlessly stand up for our values and show solidarity with people that are vulnerable. There is nothing an authoritarian leader fears more, says American professor of history and fascism Ruth Ben-Ghiat.[10]

That fear is why Trump responded to the anti-deportation protests in Los Angeles with a spectacle of brute force. It's why Orbán prosecuted the organizers of Budapest Pride in such a theatrical manner.[11] It's why anti-genocide protests are being treated with suspicion in country after country. Not because they pose a real threat to public order, but because they show the antidote to fascism: moral courage.

Showing that courage is not without consequence. It can strain your friendships, harm your career or company, or cost your party votes. And if fascism has progressed to a more advanced stage, moral courage may cost you your freedom or even your life. But there is no better option. Unchecked fascism pushes everyone and everything into the abyss, one way or another.

'If none of us is prepared to die for freedom,' Snyder notes, 'then all of us will die under tyranny.'[12] Our power lies precisely in daring to take that risk, as Palestinian journalist Mariam Barghouti explains from occupied Ramallah: 'The only way that you can stop something that is coming at full velocity is to throw yourself in front of it and try to block it… That wave of violence is gonna hit you… You have to be ready to take the hit.'[13]

Fascism is like a churning river. If you try to stop it on your own, it will drown you. But together we can raise a dam. A dam against the normalization of ideas that until recently were considered extremist. A dam that protects us from fascism breaking through. As with the age-old Dutch fight against the water, this will require the knowledge, expertise and willpower of an entire community. People who by no means agree on everything, but nonetheless share one fundamental conviction: that an attack on one person's political freedoms is an attack on the freedom of all.

Like every dam, it starts with a foundation: **politics**. Moderate parties need to secure and protect democratic ground by drawing clear boundaries and actively defending the rule of law. If the foundations are shaky, extremism will still filter into our democracies.

Then there is the protective layer of **journalism**. Journalists can help to keep the foundations intact. They make sure that facts are being heard, and form another line of defence when politicians fail to protect the boundaries. Finally, the most important part of the dam, the actual barricade: **society** itself. Citizens can push back against the anger and mistrust with which fascism floods democracy.

No two dams are the same. The shape depends on the circumstances: the force of the current, the solidity of the soil, the materials available. There is no ready-made playbook *against* fascism – no checklist that, once completed, keeps the threat out for good.

There is a vital lesson to be found in Harvard professor Erica Chenoweth's research into successful resistance movements: resist non-violently for as long as possible, and hold the line.[14] Whether you're an opposition leader, journalist or one of the millions of voters: *everyone* can contribute. Knowledge, courage, stamina and a big heart – with these, we can raise a solid dam.

But what does that mean in practice? Activists, opposition leaders and historians from countries where fascism has already breached the dam can tell us. Their experiences are a source of inspiration and guidance for building our own dam. Their acts of resistance, small and large, add up to create a politics that fights back, journalism that is resilient, and a society that holds firm.

6. The foundations: politics that fight back

Protecting democracy starts with the political system itself – any political scientist you ask will tell you this.[1] The proportional representation and multi-party systems in many European countries are far more resistant to a fascist power grab than the two-party system in the United States. Things will not spiral out of control in Europe as quickly as they have in the US.

The European culture of compromise and the fragmentation of political parties mean that the far right usually has to come to power through coalitions with moderate parties. This makes it harder to undermine the rule of law, but by no means impossible. After all, Hitler came to power with a third of the votes, through a right-wing coalition. To stop the rising tide of fascism, there are certain things that all politicians can – and should – do.

Avoid cooperation with the far right

A multi-party system provides one key advantage that Americans in their two-party system don't have: by ruling out cooperation with far-right parties, traditional parties can keep the far right small – especially if they make this clear at an early stage of fascism, when voters are more likely to see a vote for the far right as a wasted vote.

Is that undemocratic? That's what the far right claims.[2] 'Absolutely not,' Sarah de Lange says. 'Parties can choose who they work with. That's how democracy works.' Besides, voters for far-right parties are still represented in parliament. And liberal democracy isn't only about elections, it's also designed to protect everyone's rights and check state power. Parties have a duty not only to respect these fundamental rights and the institutions established to guarantee them, but to defend them.

In some countries, legal steps can be taken to exclude anti-democratic parties from politics. This is possible in Germany, for example, where in 2025 the Social Democrats deliberated proceedings to ban the AfD, which had been officially classified as a right-wing extremist group.[3] Similar legislation is also in the pipeline in the Netherlands: the proposed Law on Political Parties aims to better regulate the financing, transparency and internal organization of political parties, and offer a separate legal basis to ultimately ban anti-democratic ones.[4] Once again, this raises the question: is this undemocratic? 'Most definitely not,' says de Lange. 'You *must* want this. Otherwise democracy eventually destroys itself.'

Brazil offers an excellent example of how the law can block anti-democratic forces. After sowing doubt about the integrity of the elections he lost, former president Jair Bolsonaro staged a coup attempt – very much akin to the storming of the US Capitol in 2021. Unlike Trump, however, Bolsonaro was barred from standing for election again,[5] and has since been sentenced to twenty-seven years in prison.[6]

The democratic system and its accompanying institutions – separation of powers, a constitution, an independent judiciary, access to justice, a free press, free elections – define the political playing field, and protect democracy and the rule of law from fascist power grabs.

But Timothy Snyder warns that there can be many institutional emergency brakes and safety nets in place, but politicians have to actually use them. 'Institutions do not protect themselves. They fall one after the other unless each is defended from the beginning.'[7] The task of defending institutions falls primarily on politics.

Form a cross-party coalition

There is a common belief that opposition to fascism is a left-wing affair. That idea stems from the last century, when communist and socialist parties – along with intellectuals, churches, artists and militant groups – formed the resistance. Together with the Allies, they paid an unthinkably high price to ultimately bring down the Third Reich. Anti-fascism then disappeared from politics, retreating to the fringes, carried mainly by radical left-wing movements.[8] That's how anti-fascism acquired its persistent left-wing image.

That idea is further propelled by fascist leaders, who present themselves as simply opposing the 'radical left' – and dismiss anyone who resists them as part of the 'radical left, anti-fascist plot'. The real fault line, however, is not between right and left. It runs between democracy and its enemies.

In the Netherlands, as in many other countries, every minister, state secretary and member of parliament swears an oath of allegiance to the constitution upon taking office.[9] And the rights contained in that constitution – the right to vote, freedom of expression, equal treatment – are precisely what is threatened by fascism. By definition, every politician who has taken that oath is therefore an anti-fascist. They don't need to have an Antifa sticker slapped on their briefcase to prove it, but they do need a clear political anti-fascist strategy. After all, fascism is a strategy, so resistance to it must be one too.

This, then, is an urgent call to all parties, from left to right: form a joint front *for* our freedoms and *against* the rising tide of fascism. And make room within that front for political differences, for political debate based on values, as is right and proper in a democracy.

The Hungarian opposition parties took this to the extreme ahead of the national elections in April 2026: more than a dozen opposition parties withdrew from the race, urging their supporters to vote for Orbán's strongest challenger, the Tisza Party.[10] In a last, successful attempt to save their democracy, they set aside their political differences. This is a measure of how late the hour had become. The lesson is not to wait until debate itself becomes a luxury.

Understand it, name it and fight it

'Backsliding just went by us like a train, without anybody realizing how far it had gotten,' says Hungarian opposition politician Katalin Cseh.[11] They weren't alone in this.

Time and again, politicians are caught off guard by the fascist playbook.

'It's very important to pay attention from the very beginning,' Cseh emphasizes, 'to mobilize.' The lesson is clear: do not underestimate the danger. Understand how fascist strategies work, name them, and start fighting them as early on as possible. Do everything to prevent normalization.

Newly elected mayor of New York Zohran Mamdani appears to have taken this lesson to heart: he called Trump a 'fascist' in plain terms – even after a strangely cordial meeting with the president in the Oval Office.[12]

Protect each other

Mamdani has shown us how to do this. When Trump labelled resistance to ICE as 'potential domestic terrorism', New York's mayor stood squarely behind the immigrant community in his city. And he didn't stop there. In a viral video, he explained how New Yorkers could protect themselves against the immigration raids and how to resist them.[13] This is an example of combative politics: always protect the groups and individuals that far-right politicians turn into enemies.

The same message comes from Hungary. In the words of Katalin Cseh: 'Go to every protest, go to every march, stand right beside everybody who is being attacked, no matter if it is a group you belong to… You have to stand side by side [with] each other and help and support those who might feel isolated and alone.'[14] The more people, the stronger the resistance.

Cseh's compatriot, the MEP Klára Dobrev, went a step further. She invited the entire European Parliament to march with her in the banned Budapest Pride. 'We can have different values about same-sex marriage,' she said, 'but if you are a democrat, then you definitely are on the basis that Pride cannot be banned.'[15]

Protection must extend beyond minority groups. Forming a political front against fascism means defending fellow politicians against unfounded smears. All too often, members of the Dutch parliament just sit back when PVV leader Geert Wilders mocks colleagues from the rostrum or on X. He repeatedly insinuated a connection between 'radical Muslims' and Frans Timmermans, then leader of the GroenLinks-PvdA party (now Progressief Nederland), whom he falsely labels a 'radical left-wing Jew-hater'. The conservative NSC – which Wilders invariably calls the 'National Sabotage Club' – is according to Wilders now only supported by Hamas.[16] All elected representatives, and especially the Speaker of the House, should take these attacks seriously – regardless of any political differences. Because they undermine the actual substance of political debate.

Fight personal enrichment

No voter wants to see their taxes disappear into politicians' pockets or watch those in power enrich themselves. This is the Achilles' heel of fascist, authoritarian regimes – they say they represent 'the will of the people', but corruption and personal enrichment at citizens' expense are not what the people want.

This was the key message of the Fighting Oligarchy Tour that Democrats Bernie Sanders and Alexandria Ocasio-Cortez took across the US in 2025. 'Those with the most economic, political and technological power destroy the public good to enrich themselves, while millions of Americans pay the price,' Ocasio-Cortez said at a rally in Las Vegas.[17]

By exposing corruption in Hungary, Péter Magyar – a former insider in Orbán's Fidesz party – became the favourite for the 2026 elections. He broke away from Fidesz in a Facebook post describing the Hungarian state as 'a sugar coating that serves only two purposes: to conceal how the machinery of power operates and to amass vast fortunes'.[18]

When he then leaked recordings that revealed a huge corruption scandal, Hungarians went out in the streets en masse and Magyar topped the polls, decisively beating Orbán. The lesson: expose corruption and run a campaign on a ruthless anti-corruption agenda – that's where even the strongest authoritarian leaders lose their foothold.

Sow hope, not hate

'Hope is an essential part of an anti-authoritarian strategy. It is the antidote to a deadly fatalism,' says fascism expert Ruth Ben-Ghiat.[19] Take Russian dissident Alexei Navalny, whose optimism gave people the courage to stand up to corruption and Vladimir Putin's abuse of power – even after he was murdered.

That's why you can only fight fascism with a clear vision of the future. One that speaks to the things people actually struggle with: affordable housing, accessible healthcare, good education and a secure livelihood. Instead of telling people what you're against – the bedrock of the fascist strategy – tell them what you're for. Sow hope, not hate.

It worked in Chile in 1988, where the opposition brought down dictator Augusto Pinochet with the March for Joy.[20]

It worked in Poland in 2023, where opposition leader Donald Tusk mobilized hundreds of thousands for the Million Hearts March with a message of hope. 'The impossible has become possible,' Tusk told the crowds in Warsaw, 'when I see this sea of hearts, when I see these hundreds of thousands of smiling faces, I feel that this turning point in the history of our homeland is approaching.'[21] That is how he gave people the feeling that change was possible. And, against all expectations, Tusk won the election.

It worked in New York, where Zohran Mamdani's low-budget mayoral campaign videos showed him listening to people – linking their complaints about rents, childcare and food prices directly to concrete solutions. He convinced voters that someone was finally looking out for them.[22]

And it worked in the Netherlands, where Rob Jetten, leader of the progressive-liberal D66, narrowly beat far-right PVV leader Geert Wilders with an optimistic message about 'positive forces'.[23]

Intervene to protect and strengthen the rule of law

Be vigilant and defend democracy and the rule of law from the outset – and on every front. Fight for a free press, art, culture, justice and the right to protest. Speak out against threats to and contempt for judges, and never opportunistically vote in favour of legislation that undermines the rule of law in the hope it will later flounder in court.

That is what happened in the Netherlands in July 2025, when the NSC voted in favour of criminalizing illegal stays on the cowardly condition that the Council of State would surely strike down the amendment. They themselves should have taken responsibility.[24]

It is up to politicians to test their proposals against the framework of the rule of law. In Hungary in the early stages of Orban's power grab, this frequently went awry. 'We were not aware enough at that time,' Klára Dobrev says, admitting that whenever Orbán attacked the media, civil organizations or freedom of speech, the opposition reacted too late. And now Hungary is in a lot of trouble.[25]

In Poland, the opposition turned to the EU for help. When the PiS government dismantled the rule of law, the opposition asked the European Commission to trigger an Article 7 procedure that could suspend Poland's voting rights in the EU. In the end no formal sanctions were applied, but over 100 billion euros in subsidies were frozen, slowing the government's destructive agenda. The funds were only released after Donald Tusk was elected and presented a recovery plan.[26]

Protecting the rule of law is a core task of politics. As is improving and strengthening it. Harsh criticism of how it functions is fine – as long as the starting point is how the rule of law can be improved rather than dismantled.

7. The protective layer: resilient journalism

Fascism starts with *talk*, I wrote earlier. There's one profession that especially should heed this warning: journalists. These are people who have made critical thinking their profession, public debate their workplace, and language their tool. And they stand right on the front lines of the battle for truth which marks fascism's first strike at democracy.

This is a battle that journalists can win, but it requires a careful assessment of journalistic methods. Naturally, editors already do this constantly, asking questions such as: *Who do you choose to platform and when? What deserves journalistic attention? Will a piece put people at risk?*

Fascism confronts journalists with a specific challenge. When a democracy functions and everyone is playing by the rules, the usual methods and principles – such as a focus on news, hearing both sides, fact-checking and live reporting – work perfectly fine. But fascists are operating on an entirely different playing field than ordinary politicians. The press isn't there to hold them to account, but to help them sow confusion and amplify hatred and propaganda.

In 2019, former Trump strategist and propagandist Steve Bannon bluntly revealed the strategy: 'Flood the zone with shit.'[1] It's about hijacking everyone's attention with a torrent of tumult and untruths, while at the same time grinding down democracy.

And that is precisely what news editors are struggling with – made worse by the informal laws of the media that treat 'neutrality' as the highest journalistic good, politicians as newsworthy by definition, and political tumult even more so. A new approach is required – one that Jay Rosen, associate professor of journalism at New York University, calls 'journalism with an agenda'.[2] It asks a key question: does this piece of journalism protect the democratic rule of law, or might it unintentionally undermine it?

Embrace journalism with an agenda

Journalistic neutrality – the idea that you can describe the world without taking a position in it – is a myth. The second a journalist weighs up the facts, interprets them and presents them in a context, they are already doing just that.

It becomes a dangerous myth in times of rising fascism. Remaining neutral towards the enemies of democratic standards, facts and fundamental rights makes it difficult – if not impossible – to *defend* democratic institutions, norms and values. Worse, it gradually makes the media inadvertently complicit in the fascist attacks on journalism itself. By treating fascism as 'politics as usual', particularly in its early stages, journalists help to normalize it.

Research by political scientists in the UK and Australia has confirmed this.[3] After watching an interview with a right-wing extremist politician, viewers not only agreed more with extremist views, they also believed many others already did so. If the journalist asked critical questions, the effect was lessened, but even this cannot prevent such views from being seen as more normal and widely held.

This places a tremendous responsibility on the media's shoulders. A journalist by definition champions facts and truth, and so must uphold democratic institutions. Committing to these values means journalists are not neutral – they are playing a vital role in safeguarding democracy.

Placing the right of reply in context

Embracing journalism with an agenda means reassessing the principle of hearing 'both sides'. The notion that anyone being written about has a right of reply is understandable. It gives them the opportunity to address allegations or criticism (whether justified or not), and to admit mistakes. But when fascists are given that opportunity, it almost always turns out differently.

Think back to when the *Guardian* asked US Secretary of Defense Pete Hegseth on camera about 'Signal gate', the huge security breach at his department, uncovered by a journalist from *The Atlantic*. Rather than answering, Hegseth used the time to dismiss the journalist who had revealed the leak as a 'deceitful and highly discredited so-called journalist who is in the profession of peddling hoaxes'.[4] The opportunity for rebuttal thus became free airtime for lies.

Journalists can counterbalance this by taking a position themselves – by consciously choosing whether and how to platform a fascist politician, for example, or by not simply repeating a statement but showing how it fits into a broader anti-democratic strategy.

Be careful with live news coverage

Consider the normal journalistic practice of live reporting – for example by simply broadcasting a press conference or political debate without commentary or context. In a functioning democracy, there's usually little wrong with that: democratic politicians can be assumed to be acting in good faith. They may disagree, or even say incorrect things, but they won't abuse the opportunity in order to spread hatred, propaganda or lies.

But fascist politicians play by different rules. And then live reporting becomes a risk: there is a good chance that the journalist is being used to spread disinformation or scapegoating. Live blogs of events with a fascist in the lead role? Social media feeds packaged as 'news'? Broadcasting a fascist's 'press conference' in full? You're giving a liar a megaphone and directly piping their voice into the country's living rooms. For a fascist turns the norms and practices of journalism to his advantage – and against what those practices are meant to serve: the truth.

Journalistic forms that merely report on rallies and reproduce speeches without giving context can inadvertently become tools with which to spread lies and propaganda. So avoid those formats whenever possible, Jay Rosen advises. Speaking about Trump, he writes:

'Don't cover any speech, rally, or press conference involving the president. The risk of passing along bad information is too great. Instead, attend carefully to what he says. If you can independently verify any important news he announces, then bring that to the audience – after the verification step.'[5]

More and more editors are drawing that line. Various Dutch media outlets, for example, decided not to broadcast Geert Wilders's propaganda show about his ten-point asylum plan – the prelude to his departure from the coalition – in its entirety. Instead, they placed his demands in the broader context of his ongoing attacks on the cabinet, of which his PVV was itself a part.

But things can still go awry. The Dutch public broad-caster's live blog of 2025's NATO summit in The Hague read like a Trump fan page: he arrived at this time, ate this, slept here and said that. More pointed analysis would have been more informative: this is how NATO's secretary-general helped to normalize extortion, and this is how the European leaders participated.

Dealing with lies

The fact-check is a well-known journalistic method for avoiding untruths. Because facts don't lie, right? In a healthy democracy, it is an important, effective tool that can correct falsehoods or even change one's position. But fascists do not lie to make people believe the lie, they lie to show their disdain for facts.

Anyone fact-checking such lies without mentioning that context – the function of the lie – unintentionally legitimizes fascist rhetoric. *Donald Trump says immigrants are eating cats and dogs. Are they really?* The statement may be disproved. But the real purpose of the lie – fomenting hatred towards immigrants, showcasing power, demanding loyalty – remains unnamed. And worse, the suggestion that lingers is that *it could have been true*. As Hitler said: 'Something of even the most insolent lie will always remain and stick.' These types of lies must therefore be exposed for what they are: a systematic assault on the truth.

When fact-checking, journalists should therefore always be given room to ask: *Am I inadvertently legitimizing this lie's underlying message?* If the answer is yes, then it's better to make the strategy *behind* the lie the subject of the reporting, rather than just the facts or the lie itself. And rather than putting statements between inverted commas to indicate that something may not be true, it's more effective to explicitly mention that a lie is being spread and explain what that lie is intended to do – and then refute it.[*]

Flag perversions of meaning

Fascism always inverts the meaning of words. Stripped of their normal sense, they can be given an opposite meaning: Trump literally calls his lies 'truths' (spread on a platform dubbed Truth Social); 'freedom of expression' becomes a weapon to censor critics, ban books and silence scientists; and 'security' is used as a cover to commit violence or justify it. 'War' becomes 'peace'. And in the most extreme case, genocide is even committed under the pretext of *preventing* genocide ('Never again!').

---

[*] This is known as the 'inoculation theory'.

To dismantle these perversions of meaning, it's crucial that journalists continue to name what fascists deny or distort. So call a convicted far-right activist a convicted far-right activist rather than a 'professional activist'.[6] When power operates without checks or balances, say 'regime' instead of 'government'. And use the word 'kidnapping' instead of 'administrative detention', as the latter obscures the fact that someone has been detained without a legal basis.[7]

A good example of dismantling such obscuring language: over the course of 2025, many Dutch editors switched to the term 'genocide' to describe the violence in Gaza – although some politicians systematically refused to do so, sometimes defying their own policies, and the International Court of Justice is still weighing up the matter.[8]

Call out complicity

Fascists would stand zero chance if moderate parties didn't help to normalize their talking points and behaviour. Those who go along with fascist politicians therefore deserve as much attention in the context of emerging fascism as the fascists themselves.

When Donald Trump called journalists 'scum' and 'gutless losers' at the NATO summit in The Hague, the outgoing Dutch prime minister Dick Schoof just sat next to him and kept schtum. Even when a journalist from the Dutch newspaper *NRC* asked him about it, he refused to distance himself from Trump's words.

This is a clear example of how moderate leaders contribute to the normalization of hostility. And how journalists can and should report on it.[9] By making Schoof's silence explicit, the *NRC* journalist was holding him to account: *Does the prime minister accept Trump's characterization of journalists, or will he speak out and oppose the normalization of such language?* By consistently questioning complicit bystanders, journalists can help combat the normalization of fascists.

Protect your time, team up and choose stories that make a difference

If fascist leaders attack the media by flooding the zone with 'shit', as Bannon said, then journalistic attention becomes an even scarcer commodity. Jay Rosen advises editors to ensure their daily reporting actually reflects their editorial direction. This is how they stay sharp.[10]

Journalists can join forces – as many media outlets already do for major investigations into, for example, international capital flows or the security industry.[11] And editors can build on this. Instead of ten different outlets delivering the same news separately, they can work together and coordinate who focuses on what. This way, they can form a united front against the fascist strategy that tries to divide their attention.

Protect your time, team up and choose stories that make a difference. Sometimes that means months of investigation into corruption or mismanagement – remember, fascists are ultimately always out to enrich themselves and their cronies. It should always mean stories by and about the people fascists hit first: people of colour, religious minorities, refugees, LGBTQI+ people, the unhoused, people with disabilities. Stories that show

how these people organize and how they defend themselves. When fascists instil fear of 'the Other' and spread evil stereotypes to turn groups against one another, good journalists give 'the Other' a face. Their work should always be informed by the fact that an attack on one is an attack on all of us.

Keep in mind that fascism affects people unequally. Journalism in Western countries is still predominantly white – people from minority groups are underrepresented on editorial boards and in newsrooms.[12] As a journalist, if you think fascism isn't that bad, you probably belong to the privileged group that hasn't been hit yet.

Be alert to self-censorship

Fascists have an arsenal of weapons to bully the free press: threats, troll armies, legal intimidation, buying up media and cutting off funding.[13] This creates an atmosphere of fear that can lead to self-censorship.

Resist that reflex. Never obey those in power in advance. If you know you're right, don't water down your words for fear of retaliation. Join forces to protect yourself against hate campaigns and lawsuits. Support other journalists who are facing tactics of intimidation. Establish a legal fund. Take as your role models those who never succumb to threats or harassment. Before you know it, it will no longer be a choice.

8. The barrier: society in solidarity

Fascism gets its chance because people keep telling themselves *it can't happen here*. And even when it does, many convince themselves it is already too late to act.

This is what Black American civil-rights activist Eric K. Ward calls the 'Other Big Lie': the idea that we are 'helpless and hopeless' against fascism.[1] That lie is how we look away. While Muslims, Black people, trans people and other groups in society are discriminated against. While refugees are pushed into conditions no human being should endure. While our governments back the genocide of the Palestinian people.

That idea of powerlessness is dangerous. It replaces solidarity with self-centeredness and moral courage with dull indifference. It keeps authoritarian leaders firmly in the saddle. After World War II, Jewish German-American philosopher and historian Hannah Arendt stated that a society in which people become alienated from each other is the most vulnerable to authoritarianism: 'Totalitarian movements are mass organizations of atomized, isolated individuals.'[2]

Ever wonder if you would have resisted the Nazis during World War II? The answer lies in what you do against rising fascism *today*. Do you look the other way, or do you speak up? For, as Arendt warned: 'The sad truth is that most evil is done by people who never make up their minds to be good or evil.'[3]

The strongest barrier against fascism is our refusal to participate in its hatred and dehumanization. You don't have to be a professional activist to help raise it. Nor should you just leave it to journalists or politicians. Resistance is about how people think and act. That is our starting point and that's where each of us has a choice to make. Don't be a bystander. Become an upstander.

Start with yourself

Fascism slashes norm after norm. From compliance with international law to constitutional equality, from deference to the courts to debates grounded in facts: under fascism, these pillars are torn down one by one. 'There is no such thing as static extremism,' Jewish American critic Elad Nehorai says. 'Unless it is stopped, extremism gets more extreme.'[4] So stop it. Protect human dignity.

Open your heart and care for your fellow humans. If you listen to the stories of people who have been affected by fascism, its consequences are no longer abstract. You feel the hunger and pain of a Palestinian child. The fear and insecurity of Muslims, migrants or trans people. The exhaustion of journalists and writers facing troll armies, lawsuits and death threats for doing their job. And you will feel it: *their freedom is also mine.*

Our shared humanity fuels anger against the system causing that suffering. A 'Rebellion of Care', as American poet David Gate calls it.[5] This rebellion moves people to organize. Communities form a wall to protect neighbours from immigration raids, like they did in Los Angeles or Minneapolis. Civil servants, police officers or immigration officials stand up for the constitution against their own government, as officials from the Dutch Ministry of Foreign Affairs have done – protesting against the lack of political action against Israel every week since December 2023.[6] Activists are willing to take the blows and be prosecuted as 'terrorists', as is now happening in the UK. These are all expressions of that shared humanity – or, in Gate's words, 'empathy with a backbone'.[7]

Avoid violence

Fascism is beaten by numbers, as research by Harvard professor Erica Chenoweth shows. To successfully resist the onset of fascism, anyone must be willing *and* able to participate – and non-violence is a necessary condition for this, for as long as it is possible. More importantly, by rejecting violence, you demonstrate a better alternative. Non-violent resistance, as Martin Luther King Jr. wrote in 1958, 'is not unrealistic submission to evil power. It is rather a courageous confrontation of evil by the power of love.'[8]

Weigh your words

'Be kind to our language,' Timothy Snyder urges.[9] Because fascists appropriate the meaning of words in order to wipe out critical thinking.

Under the guise of 'free speech', Trump announced sweeping measures to silence progressives after the murder of right-wing conservative activist Charlie Kirk.[10] And under the guise of protecting specific groups in society, other minority groups are threatened. By carelessly adopting the language of fascists – saying 'war' instead of 'genocide', 'free speech' instead of 'censorship' – you not only reinforce their framing, you let them inside your own thinking.

Stay curious about other people

Language shapes how we see reality, but just as important is opening ourselves up to the ideas, knowledge and experiences of others, including those who think differently. Fascists stoke an 'us vs them' dynamic through propaganda that fans distrust and disrupts public debate; curiosity is the best counter to this. And yes, that also means staying curious about the reasoning of people who vote for fascist politicians.

Studies in the Netherlands, Austria and France show that people living near a new asylum accommodation facility develop a more positive attitude towards asylum seekers, which then translates into a sharp decline in support for far-right parties.[11] The best remedy for scapegoat tactics is simply human contact.

You can actively seek it out. The volunteers of Deep Canvassing Netherlands do exactly this, working with a method inspired by US political campaign strategies. The gist is simple: knock on a neighbour's door to talk about a topic that divides society.[12]

These conversations follow a fixed pattern. The volunteer takes a position, then listens to the other person's story and asks about the experiences and emotions behind it. Contradictions are named and explored, to understand how someone arrived at their view. Finally, the volunteer shares their own perspective or personal story. Research into these kinds of conversations – for example, about trans rights – shows that they effectively and sustainably contribute to greater empathy towards 'the Other'.[13]

Protect critical thinking in society

Public debate is human contact at scale. A healthy public debate creates the space to engage with dissenters and break down feelings of distrust of 'the Other'. That is precisely why fascists take aim at the pillars supporting that debate at an early stage: media, bookstores, cultural institutions, universities and human rights organizations.

This, too, is something you can resist. Immerse yourself in new scientific insights. Read novels and poetry. Share journalism that matters. And if you can: pay for independent media, support museums, donate to charities. 'Then you will have made a free choice that supports civil society and helps others to do good,' Timothy Snyder says in *On Tyranny*.

Have fun

American activist Keya Chatterjee engages her neighbours not to change their opinions, but to mobilize her community against Trump. She organizes community gatherings, crafting clubs and block parties, to bring people together and prime them for action. 'Trump says he's President of the Kennedy Center even though he's never been there because he doesn't like drag performances? We put on a rocking drag performance in the street because this is OUR HOUSE,' she says.[14] Chatterjee's priority is not resistance, it's joy. And joy serves as an antidote to the fear that authoritarian leaders try to sow – and an attractive reason for that much-needed human contact.

Fascism expert Ruth Ben-Ghiat endorses this: 'Positive emotions such as love, solidarity, and yes, joy, have been part of successful anti-authoritarian political strategies. Positive emotions motivate people to engage in politics when they might have grown apathetic or cynical about the possibility of change.'[15]

Form a network

Where Chatterjee focuses on her community of neighbours, Ami Fields-Meyer – former adviser to then US vice president Kamala Harris – points to the need for building a community of ideas: a 'political home' where shared beliefs can form the basis for collective action.[16] You don't need a detailed political vision to build one. His advice: 'If there's an issue which is drawing you in – healthcare, climate, abortion, economic development, civil rights, the Middle East, homelessness, food insecurity, local races – start there. Call someone you know who seems to be connected to the issue and say – listen, I don't totally get what it is you do but I'd like to learn. Where should I go?'

Or do as the band Massive Attack did: build your political home yourself. In response to 'aggressive, vexatious campaigns', intimidations, legal charges and new festival policies to silence artists speaking out against the genocide in Gaza during their performances, they teamed up with other acts to start an alliance – with more established performers helping budding artists.[17]

This is how you build a network of like-minded people. And several of these networks can together grow into a broad coalition that forms a real force of opposition.

Hit the streets

Neighbourly contact and political networks help, but street protests are also a must. Think of the No Kings protests, which have taken across the US, or the recurring demonstrations for Palestine around the world.

Protest doesn't have to be large: you can raise a flag, put up stickers, or wear symbolic expressions of solidarity. It is important to be clear that you do not accept any restriction of political freedom. Fascists may say they represent the will of the people, but mass resistance shows that the people actually want the opposite. You can't leave it all up to politicians – and it cannot wait until the next election.

Make your vote count

As I wrote earlier: fascism begins with elections, not with a coup. And the voting booth is also where resistance takes place. Think of your ballot as a sandbag when the dam is about to breach – and every sandbag counts. Use that opportunity.

One in five eligible Dutch voters still stays home on national election day.[18] Americans vote at even lower rates – one in three does not cast a ballot in the presidential elections,[19] on par with the European average.[20] For European Parliament elections, voter turnout drops to roughly one in two.[21] We cannot afford to be this indifferent. Talk about the need to vote with your children, your parents, your friends, your colleagues. Weigh your words and stay curious about each other. Fascism can only be fought together.

Vote for a party that suits you – just don't vote for a fascist. Perhaps you've grown used to the conspiracy theorists in politics, to the hatemongers, to the loudmouths tearing down public debate with lies big or small. Perhaps you think this inflammatory talk is pure election rhetoric, and that real power will bring a sense of responsibility. Perhaps you think, in short, that it can't happen here. Until it does just that.

This is how it works. This is fascism.

Acknowledgements

We owe our knowledge about fascism and authoritarianism to the groundbreaking work of political scientists, historians, legal scholars, and philosophers from whose research I have drawn abundantly. I am particularly indebted to the work of (in no particular order): Robert Paxton, Roger Griffin, Jason Stanley, Timothy Snyder, Ruth Ben-Ghiat, M. Gessen, Naomi Klein, Hannah Arendt, Anne Applebaum, Steven Levitsky, Jay Rosen, Daniel Ziblatt and Larry Bartels. I stand on their shoulders, but the analysis, that *this* is indeed fascism, is my own.

Special thanks to professors Federico Finchelstein, Catherine de Vries, Sarah de Lange, Matthijs Rooduijn, Hanneke van Eijken, Thomas Weber and researcher Jelle Postma, who generously gave their time to share their expertise on contemporary politics, democracy and fascism – past and present.

I based this book on public statements by politicians and their supporters. They made these on their own social media channels and websites, during press conferences and debates, and in party programmes or policy documents, and they were recorded by many observant journalists. My profound thanks to all those colleagues in Europe and the US: only through their tireless reporting was I able to expose the patterns.

I could never have written this book without the insights of journalists, human rights activists, opposition leaders and countless other people across the world who showed me how to resist oppression and violence. They let me learn from them in Sudan, South Sudan, the Democratic Republic of Congo, Rwanda, Burundi, Kenya, Palestine, Israel and Iran. Their courage and commitment to justice are a lasting inspiration to me. Together, we will hold the line.

I'm especially grateful to my colleagues at the Dutch journalism platform *De Correspondent*. It's a privilege to have you in my corner. This book started with you. A special mention to Milou Klein Lankhorst, Andreas Jonkers, Rob Wijnberg, Rinke Verkerk, Jelmer Mommers, Femke Gehoel, Veerle Schyns, Rosanne Kropman and Dieuwke van Wijk. With your faith in this book and your practical support, you all proved: no one faces fascism alone – even when only writing about it.

Thanks to Erica Moore, who translated my earlier article on this topic and whose work I gratefully drew on here and there. To my publisher Shoaib Rokadiya, my brilliant copy-editor Gemma Wain and everyone at Atlantic Books: thanks to you all, my book can reach as far as the global phenomenon it describes.

I wrote this book about hate out of love. Love for all the people, big and small, who are so dear to me. Because the freedom of all means your freedom too.

Notes

Introduction

1. The White House [@WhiteHouse], 'ASMR: Illegal Alien Deportation Flight https://t.co/O6L1iYt9b4', X (formerly Twitter), 18 February 2025, https://x.com/WhiteHouse/status/1891922058415603980.
2. PBS NewsHour, 'WATCH: Harris Calls Trump a "Fascist" in CNN Town Hall', YouTube, 24 October 2024, https://www.youtube.com/watch?v=wO0fglSeaYc.
3. M. Yang, '"Fascist", "Conman", "Predator", "Cheat": What 11 Former Trump Staffers Say about Him Now', *The Guardian*, 25 October 2024, https://www.theguardian.com/us-news/2024/oct/25/election-trump-staffers-john-kelly.
4. M. Shore, T. Snyder and J. Stanley, 'We Study Fascism, and We're Leaving the U.S.', *The New York Times*, 14 May 2025, https://www.nytimes.com/video/opinion/100000010157022/yale-canada-fascism.html. In October 2025, Rutgers professor of history Mark Bray, an Antifa specialist, fled the US after receiving death threats. A. Kassam, 'Death Threats and Accusations: The Professor Targeted by the US Far Right', *The Guardian*, 18 November 2025, https://www.theguardian.com/us-news/2025/nov/18/death-threats-and-accusations-the-professor-targeted-by-the-us-far-right.
5. Read the open letter at stopreturnfascism.org.
6. For a much-discussed US example, see: E. Bradner, 'Trump Calls Harris a Fascist, Says He Is "the Opposite of a Nazi"', CNN Politics, 19 October 2024, https://edition.cnn.com/2024/10/28/politics/donald-trump-kamala-harris-fascist.
7. Historian Ruth Ben-Giath reveals the similarities between different authoritarian currents ranging from Adolf Hitler's fascist regime in Germany to Idi Amin's military dictatorship in Uganda. R. Ben-Ghiat, *Strongmen: Mussolini to the Present*, New York, Norton, 2021.
8. In his *The Wannabe Fascists: A Guide to Understanding the Greatest*

Threat to Democracy (2024), historian Federico Finchelstein shows how twentieth-century fascism and post-war populism are now merging into a novel variant of fascism.

9. On 16 November 2025, *Atlantic* staff writer Tom Nichols posted a thread along these lines on Bluesky: 'If America were fascist right now, I would not be posting here. Neither would you.' In an interview with Dutch newspaper *NRC* on 18 December 2025, populism expert Cas Mudde said: 'I don't believe it is a fascist country. If it was, millions of people would not have been able to take to the streets during the recent No Kings demonstrations. In fascist countries, you'd get beaten up. Here there was no police brutality.'

10. In July 2004, the International Court of Justice ruled that the Israeli occupation and settlements in the Palestinian territories violate international law, and that Israel must stop construction and make reparations. The verdict can be read on the United Nations website: 'International Court of Justice finds Israeli barrier in Palestinian territory is illegal', 9 July 2004, https://news.un.org/en/story/2004/07/108912.

11. International Rescue Committee, 'Crisis in Sudan: What Is Happening and How to Help', 9 January 2026, https://www.rescue.org/article/crisis-sudan-what-happening-and-how-help.

12. World Food Programme, 'Emergency: Sudan', https://www.wfp.org/emergencies/sudan, accessed 20 January 2026.

13. There were almost 6 million casualties. See: The Center for Preventive Action, 'Conflict in the Democratic Republic of Congo', Global Conflict Tracker, 16 December 2025, https://cfr.org/global-conflict-tracker/conflict/violence-democratic-republic-congo.

14. S. McCammon, 'Donald Trump Has Brought On Countless Controversies in an Unlikely Campaign', NPR, 5 November 2016, https://www.npr.org/2016/11/05/500782887/donald-trumps-road-to-election-day.

15. USA for UNHCR, 'Refugee Crisis in Europe: Aid, Statistics and News', https://www.unrefugees.org/emergencies/europe/, accessed 20 January 2026.

16. T. Snyder, *Bloodlands: Europe between Hitler and Stalin*, New York, Basic Books, 2010.

17. See, for instance: R. O. Paxton, *The Anatomy of Fascism*, New York, Knopf, 2004.

18. R. Griffin, *The Nature of Fascism*, New York, St. Martin's Press, 1991.

19. R. Griffin, *Fascism: An Introduction to Comparative Fascist Studies*, Cambridge, Polity Press, 2018, p. 60.

20. Robert O. Paxton defines it as follows, 'Fascism may be

defined as a form of political behavior marked by obsessive preoccupation with community decline, humiliation, or victimhood and by compensatory cults of unity, energy, and purity, in which a mass-based party of committed nationalist militants, working in uneasy but effective collaboration with traditional elites, abandons democratic liberties and pursues with redemptive violence and without ethical or legal restraints goals of internal cleansing and external expansion.' *The Anatomy of Fascism*, p. 218.

1. The fascist playbook

1. A. Césaire, *Discourse on Colonialism*, trans. Joan Pinkham, with Robin D. G. Kelley, New York, Monthly Review Press, 2000. First published in French in 1950.
2. B. Mussolini, 'The doctrine of fascism', *Ideals and Ideologies*, London, Routledge, 2019, p. 342. Published under Mussolini's name but written by scholars sympathetic to fascism, this originally appeared in the *Enciclopedia Italiana* in 1932.
3. F. Finchelstein, *The Wannabe Fascists: A Guide to Understanding the Greatest Threat to Democracy*, Oakland, University of California Press, 2024.
4. U. Eco, *How to Spot a Fascist*, London, Harvill Secker, 2020. His first essay on the subject, 'Ur-fascism', appeared in *The New York Review of Books* in June 1995.
5. T. Snyder, 'What Does It Mean That Donald Trump Is a Fascist?', *The New Yorker*, 8 November 2024, https://www.newyorker.com/magazine/dispatches/ what-does-it-mean-that-donald-trump-is-a-fascist.
6. The term 'neofascism' denotes post-war forms of fascism inspired by Nazism. Britannica Editors, 'Neofascism,' *Encyclopedia Britannica*, 21 February 2025, https://www.britannica.com/topic/neofascism.
7. A Russian form of fascism sees 'actual fascists calling their opponents "fascists", blaming the Holocaust on the Jews, treating the Second World War as an argument for more violence.' T. Snyder, *The Road to Unfreedom: Russia, Europe, America*, London, Tim Duggan Books, 2018.
8. The term 'hedofascism' was introduced by cultural philosopher Thijs Lijster to show how pleasure is key to the contemporary form of fascism which revolves around maintaining one's lifestyle of excessive consumption and whose main political battle is to ensure the continued dominance of white men. T. Lijster,

'Hedofascisme: Ideologie van het ongebreidelde verlangen', *De Groene Amsterdammer*, 21 May 2025, https://www.groene.nl/artikel/ideologie-van-het-ongebreidelde-verlangen.

9. Journalist Ece Temelkuran has written about 'cloud fascism' and how it highlights the technological and transnational side of contemporary fascism. 'Cloud fascism has infinite hands committing unpredictable crimes with the randomness that we all try to catch up with and adapt to.' E. Temelkuran, 'Can the Term "Cloud Fascism" Help Us Understand – and Resist – the Hard Right?', *The Guardian*, 10 May 2025, https://www.theguardian.com/commentisfree/2025/may/10/cloud-fascism-understand-resist-hard-right.

10. Naomi Klein and Astra Taylor use the phrase 'end times fascism' to highlight the role of tech oligarchs and fascism's interconnectedness with the climate crisis. 'End times fascism is a darkly festive fatalism – a final refuge for those who find it easier to celebrate destruction than imagine living without supremacy.' N. Klein and A. Taylor, 'The Rise of End Times Fascism', *The Guardian*, 13 April 2025, https://www.theguardian.com/us-news/ng-interactive/2025/apr/13/end-times-fascism-far-right-trump-musk.

11. Federico Finchelstein describes 'wannabe fascism' as a new political phenomenon in which democratically elected populist leaders (such as Trump, Bolsonaro and Modi) adopt the core tools of fascism – xenophobia, propaganda and political intimidation or violence – to undermine democracy from within. They're not (yet) establishing a complete dictatorship, but they do create a dangerous aspirational form of fascism mainly aiming to erode and destroy democratic norms, rather than seeking total control as in historical fascism. Finchelstein, *The Wannabe Fascists*.

12. Mussolini, 'The doctrine of fascism,' p. 342.

13. Paxton, *The Anatomy of Fascism*.

14. D. Tourish, 'It is time to use the F word about Trump: Fascism, populism and the rebirth of history', *Leadership*, vol. 20, no. 1, 2023, pp. 9–32.

15. Finchelstein, *The Wannabe Fascists*.

16. According to research by political psychologist Karen Stenner, author of the book *The Authoritarian Dynamic* (2005), about 30 per cent of people in liberal democracies have an 'authoritarian predisposition': a deep sensitivity to scapegoating and strong leadership. That sensitivity only gets stronger in times of crisis. K. Stenner, 'Authoritarianism', HOPE not hate, 1 November 2020, https://hopenothate.org.uk/2020/11/01/authoritarianism/.

17. Larry M. Bartels, *Democracy Erodes from the Top: Leaders, Citizens, and the Challenge of Populism in Europe*, Princeton, Princeton University Press, 2023.

18. Paxton, *The Anatomy of Fascism*.

19. A. Hermes and H. Klüver, 'Taming the Far Right? Government Inclusion Strengthens Rather than Weakens Far-Right Parties', preprint, SocArXiv, 13 November 2025, https://doi.org/10.31235/osf.io/3mtxs_v1.

20. D. Bolet and F. Foos, 'Media Platforming and the Normalisation of Extreme Right Views', *British Journal of Political Science*, 55, 2025, e103, https://doi.org/10.1017/S0007123425000195.

21. 'And so tyranny naturally arises out of democracy, and the most aggravated form of tyranny and slavery out of the most extreme form of liberty.' Plato, *The Republic*, Book VIII, translated by Benjamin Jowett.

22. J. Goebbels, 'Die Dummheit der Demokratie,' in *Der Angriff. Aufsätze aus der Kampfzeit*, ed. Hans Schwarz van Berk, München, Zentralverlag der NSDAP, Franz Eher Nachf., 1935, p. 61.

23. As Finchelstein writes: 'Wannabe fascists tend to downgrade democracy, curtailing freedom and rights, sometimes even through attempted resurrection – but eventually they cop out.' Finchelstein, *The Wannabe Fascists*, p. 169.

24. F. Zakaria, 'The Rise of Illiberal Democracy', *Foreign Affairs*, vol. 76, no. 6, 1997, pp. 22–43; S. Levitsky and L. A. Way, *Competitive Authoritarianism: Hybrid Regimes after the Cold War*, Cambridge, Cambridge University Press, 2010.

25. Eco, *How to Spot a Fascist*.

26. R. O. Paxton, 'The Five Stages of Fascism', *The Journal of Modern History*, vol. 70, no. 1, 1998, pp. 1–23.

27. J. Stanley, *How Fascism Works: The Politics of Us and Them*, New York, Random House, 2018.

28. Cited in Stanley, *How Fascism Works*, p. 13.

29. Adolf Hitler, *Mein Kampf*, trans. Ralph Manheim, Houghton Mifflin Company, 1943, https://archive.org/details/in.ernet.dli.2015.54153/page/231/mode/2up.

30. Hitler, *Mein Kampf*.

31. Eco, *How to Spot a Fascist*.

32. J. Kallestrup and M. Michelini, 'Why Demagogues Lie Big', in *Episteme*, Cambridge University Press, 2025.

33. M. Gessen, *Surviving Autocracy*, London, Granta, 2020.

34. He attributed this strategy to an international Jewish elite and other enemies, only to then use it himself.

35. Hitler, *Mein Kampf*.

36. Snyder, 'What Does It Mean That Donald Trump Is a Fascist?'
37. A. Hitler, *Sämtliche Aufzeichnungen: 1905–1924*, edited by Eberhard Jäckel and Axel Kuhn. Stuttgart, 1980.
38. Hitler, *Mein Kampf*.
39. R. Ben-Ghiat, 'Fascist Population Engineering: Yes to White Christian Births, No to Immigrants and LGBTQ Families', *Lucid*, Substack newsletter, 2 May 2025, https://lucid.substack.com/p/fascist-population-engineering-yes.
40. Paxton, *The Anatomy of Fascism*.
41. G. Aly, *Hitler's Beneficiaries: Plunder, Racial War, and the Nazi Welfare State*, New York, Henry Holt, 2007.
42. See, for example: Chris Wetton, *Hitler's Fortune*, Barnsley, Pen and Sword Military, 2004.
43. 'Official Party Statement on Its Attitude Toward the Farmers and Agriculture', in B. M. Lane and L. J. Rupp, *Nazi Ideology Before 1933*, Austin, University of Texas Press, 1978, p. 118–23. Cited in: Stanley, *How Fascism Works*, p. 105.
44. R. J. B. Bosworth, *Mussolini's Italy: Life Under the Fascist Dictatorship, 1915–1945*, New York, Penguin Books, 2005.
45. T. W. Ryback, 'How Hitler Dismantled a Democracy in 53 Days', *The Atlantic*, 8 January 2025, https://www.theatlantic.com/ideas/archive/2025/01/hitler-germany-constitution-authoritarianism/681233/.
46. Finchelstein, *The Wannabe Fascists*.

2. Fascism has a new face: the Trump regime

1. R. O. Paxton, 'I've Hesitated to Call Donald Trump a Fascist. Until Now', *Newsweek*, 11 January 2021, https://www.newsweek.com/robert-paxton-trump-fascist-1560652, accessed 20 January 2026.
2. E. Zerofsky, 'Is It Fascism? A Leading Historian Changes His Mind', *The New York Times Magazine*, 23 October 2024, https://www.nytimes.com/2024/10/23/magazine/robert-paxton-facism.html.
3. N. Layne, 'Trump repeats "poisoning the blood" anti-immigrant remark', *Reuters*, December 17, 2023 https://www.reuters.com/world/us/trump-repeats-poisoning-blood-anti-immigrant-remark-2023-12-16/.
4. G. Kessler, S. Rizzo and M. Kelly, 'Trump's false or misleading claims total 30,573 over 4 years', *The Washington Post*, 24 January 2021, https://www.washingtonpost.com/politics/2021/01/24/trumps-false-or-misleading-claims-total-30573-over-four-years/.

5. A. Gomez Licon, 'Trump Was Challenged after Blaming DEI for the DC Plane Crash. Here's What He Said', AP News, 30 January 2025, https://apnews.com/article/plane-crash-washington-dc-trump-dei-claims-3ac5486ec594d81e919e8ebbd9733869.

6. D. Dale, 'Fact Check: Trump Falsely Claims Schools Are Secretly Sending Children for Gender-Affirming Surgeries', CNN, 4 September 2024, https://www.cnn.com/2024/09/04/politics/donald-trump-fact-check-children-gender-affirming-surgery.

7. M. Thomas and M. Wendling, 'Donald Trump Repeats Baseless Claim about Haitian Immigrants Eating Cats and Dogs in Springfield, Ohio', BBC News, 15 September 2024, https://www.bbc.com/news/articles/c77l28myezko.

8. M. Murphy and J. Horton, 'Fact-Checking Donald Trump's Claims about War in Ukraine', BBC News, 19 February 2025, https://www.bbc.com/news/articles/c9814k2jlxko.

9. Reporters Without Borders, 'Trump's War on the Press: 10 Numbers from the US President's First 100 Days', 25 April 2025, https://rsf.org/en/trump-s-war-press-10-numbers-us-president-s-first-100-days.

10. H. Lewis, 'A White House Briefing Straight from North Korea', *The Atlantic*, 2 May 2025, https://www.theatlantic.com/ideas/archive/2025/05/maga-influencers-press-new-media/682666/.

11. E. Berger, 'Pentagon Names New Press Corps from Far-Right Outlets after Reporter Walkout', *The Guardian*, 22 October 2025, https://www.theguardian.com/us-news/2025/oct/22/pentagon-press-corps.

12. S. Levitsky, L. Way and D. Ziblatt, 'How Will We Know When We Have Lost Our Democracy?', *New York Times*, 8 May 2025, https://www.nytimes.com/2025/05/08/opinion/trump-authoritarianism-democracy.html, accessed 20 January 2026.

13. D. J. Trump, 'Continuing the Reduction of the Federal Bureaucracy', The White House, 15 March 2025, https://www.whitehouse.gov/presidential-actions/2025/03/continuing-the-reduction-of-the-federal-bureaucracy/.

14. N. Ulaby, 'Trump Expands "woke" Criticism from Smithsonian to Other Museums', NPR, 19 August 2025, https://www.npr.org/2025/08/19/nx-s1-5507221/trump-smithsonian-museums-woke.

15. C. de Guzman, '"A Dark Moment for America": Trump Responds to Charlie Kirk's Death', *Time*, 11 September 2025, https://time.com/7316299/charlie-kirk-shot-death-donald-trump-speech-transcript-political-violence/.

16. D. J. Trump, 'Designating Antifa as a Domestic Terrorist

Organization', The White House, 22 September 2025, https://www.whitehouse.gov/presidential-actions/2025/09/ designating-antifa-as-a-domestic-terrorist-organization/.

17. This wave of dismissals of people critical of Charlie Kirk went far beyond the media. Wikipedia offers a comprehensive overview: https://en.wikipedia.org/wiki/Reprisals_against_commentators_ on_the_Charlie_Kirk_assassination.

18. Wikipedia offers a non-exhaustive overview of the conspiracy theories Trump has spread: https://en.wikipedia.org/wiki/ List_of_conspiracy_theories_promoted_by_Donald_Trump.

19. Z. Kanno-Youngs and S. McCreesh, 'Trump Calls Somalis "Garbage" He Doesn't Want in the Country', *The New York Times*, 2 December 2025, https://www.nytimes.com/2025/12/02/us/ politics/trump-somalia.html.

20. O. Alafriz, '"Poisoning the Blood of Our Country": Trump Delivers Caustic Attack on Immigrants', *Politico*, 16 December 2023, https://www.politico.com/news/2023/12/16/trump-immigration-attack-00132156, accessed 20 January 2026.

21. Donald J. Trump, 'Establishing Project Homecoming', The White House, 9 May 2025, https://www.whitehouse.gov/presidential-actions/2025/05/establishing-project-homecoming/, accessed 20 January 2026.

22. S. Hubbard, 'ICE to Use ImmigrationOS by Palantir, a New AI System, to Track Immigrants' Movements', American Immigration Council, 21 August 2025, https://www.americanimmigrationcouncil.org/blog/ ice-immigrationos-palantir-ai-track-immigrants/.

23. The White House [@WhiteHouse], 'Illegal aliens, we repeat: SELF-DEPORT NOW OR FACE ENORMOUS FINANCIAL PENALTIES AND DEPORTATION. https://t.co/ fXV33VoEWc', X, 10 May 2025, https://x.com/WhiteHouse/ status/1920995563861889176.

24. K. Iyer, 'US Will Reexamine All Green Cards Issued to People from 19 Countries as Trump Administration Ramps up Immigration Crackdown', CNN, 27 November 2025, https://www.cnn.com/2025/11/27/politics/ us-reexamining-green-card-holders-19-countries.

25. R. Payne, 'ICE's $175 Billion Windfall: Trump's Mass Deportation Force Set to Receive Military-Level Funding', *Salon*, 3 July 2025, https://www.salon.com/2025/07/03/ ices-175-billion-windfall-trumps-mass-deportation-force-set-to-receive-military-level-funding/.

26. F. Chothia, 'Are White South Africans Facing a Genocide as

Donald Trump Claims?', BBC News, 2 June 2025, https://www.bbc.com/news/articles/c9wg5pg1xp5o.

27. S. Patrick, 'Trump Has Launched a Second American Revolution. This Time, It's Against the World', Emissary – Carnegie Endowment for International Peace, 19 March 2025, https://carnegieendowment.org/emissary/2025/03/trump-foreign-policy-second-american-revolution-nato-un?lang=en.

28. The White House, *National Security Strategy of the United States of America*, November 2025, https://www.whitehouse.gov/wp-content/uploads/2025/12/2025-National-Security-Strategy.pdf.

29. The White House, *National Security Strategy of the United States of America*.

30. J. Landale and R. Hagan, 'Trump Says US Needs Greenland after Naming Special Envoy', BBC News, 22 December 2025, https://www.bbc.com/news/articles/ckgmd132ge4o.

31. D. J. Trump, 'Imposing Sanctions on the International Criminal Court', The White House, 6 February 2025, https://www.whitehouse.gov/presidential-actions/2025/02/imposing-sanctions-on-the-international-criminal-court/.

32. Office of the Spokesperson, US Department of State, 'Withdrawal from Wasteful, Ineffective, or Harmful International Organizations', press statement, 7 January 2026, https://www.state.gov/releases/office-of-the-spokesperson/2026/01/withdrawal-from-wasteful-ineffective-or-harmful-international-organizations/.

33. K. Epstein, 'USAID in Turmoil as Trump and Musk Aim to Shut down Aid Agency', BBC News, 4 February 2025, https://www.bbc.com/news/articles/cdjdmx12j9no.

34. Z. Palomo, 'Trump Brags That Friend Charles Schwab Made $2bn from Stock Market Chaos', *Independent*, 11 April 2025, https://www.independent.co.uk/tv/news/trump-charles-schwab-stock-market-tariffs-nascar-b2731568.html.

35. The White House, *National Security Strategy of the United States of America*.

36. W. Weissert, J. Cappelletti and R. Garcia Cano, 'Venezuela's Machado says she presented her Nobel Peace Prize to Trump during their meeting', Associated Press, 16 January 2026, https://apnews.com/article/trump-machado-venezuela-maduro-nobel-peace-prize-ed23992bccabf128b7e849259d3c29a8.

37. S. Lawal, 'How Many Countries Has Trump Bombed in 2025?', Al Jazeera, 31 December 2025, https://www.aljazeera.com/news/2025/12/31/how-many-countries-has-trump-bombed-in-2025.

38. J. Gedeon, 'Trump Administration Launches Portal for Reporting DEI in Public Schools', *The Guardian*, 27 February 2025, https://www.theguardian.com/us-news/2025/feb/27/trump-administration-dei-reporting-website.

39. S. Anderson, 'A Key Part of Trump's Immigration Plan: Urge Americans to Snitch', *Forbes*, 20 January 2025, https://www.forbes.com/sites/stuartanderson/2025/01/20/a-key-part-of-trumps-immigration-plan-urge-americans-to-snitch/.

40. K. Yourish et al., 'These Words Are Disappearing in the New Trump Administration', *The New York Times*, 7 March 2025, https://www.nytimes.com/interactive/2025/03/07/us/trump-federal-agencies-websites-words-dei.html.

41. R. Ben-Ghiat, 'Fascist Population Engineering'.

42. The White House, *National Security Strategy of the United States of America*.

43. Q. Slobodian, 'Maga's Sinister Obsession with IQ Is Leading Us towards an Inhuman Future', *The Guardian*, 28 April 2025, https://www.theguardian.com/commentisfree/2025/apr/28/maga-iq-inhuman-future-intelligence-ai.

44. The White House, *National Security Strategy of the United States of America*.

45. A. Choi and D. Gainor, 'Analyzing the Scale of Trump's Federal Layoffs in His First 100 Days', CNN, 26 April 2025, https://www.cnn.com/2025/04/26/politics/federal-layoffs-trump-musk-dg.

46. As frequently communicated through the DOGE website.

47. B. Green, 'DOGE Plan to Push AI Across the US Federal Government Is Wildly Dangerous', *Tech Policy Press*, 6 March 2025, https://techpolicy.press/doge-plan-to-push-ai-across-the-us-federal-government-is-wildly-dangerous.

48. R. Brownstein, 'Trump Is About to Betray His Rural Supporters', *The Atlantic*, 13 December 2024, https://www.theatlantic.com/politics/archive/2024/12/trump-gop-rural-supporters/680981.

49. R. Leingang, 'The Rightwing Plan to Take over "Sanctuary" Cities – and Rebuild Them Maga-Style', *The Guardian*, 26 May 2024, https://www.theguardian.com/us-news/article/2024/may/26/trump-project-2025-sanctuary-cities.

50. B. Johansen and S. Kapos, '"This Is Not a Joke": Chicago Leaders Slam Trump after President Declares "Chipocalypse Now"', *Politico*, 8 Sept. 2025, https://www.politico.com/news/2025/09/06/trump-chicago-ice-war-00548817.

51. I. Sentner, 'Trump Places DC Police under Federal Control, Deploys National Guard', *Politico*, 11 August 2025, https://www.politico.com/news/2025/08/11/trump-dc-police-federal-control-00502708.

52. M. Ward, 'Trump's National Guard Deployments Are Part of a Broader Immigration Plan', *Politico*, 4 September 2025, https://www.politico.com/news/2025/09/04/trumps-blue-city-law-and-order-crackdowns-are-also-about-immigration-00544545.

53. M. S. Schmidt and M. Cullen, 'A List of Those Who Could Be in Line for Trump's "Retribution"', *The New York Times*, 18 January 2025, https://www.nytimes.com/2025/01/18/us/politics/trump-retribution-list.html.

54. E. Bumiller and E. L. Green, 'Trump Fires Black Officials from an Overwhelmingly White Administration', *The New York Times*, 8 October 2025, https://www.nytimes.com/2025/10/08/us/politics/black-leaders-trump.html.

55. P. Stone, '"Hallmarks of Authoritarianism": Trump Banks on Loyalists as He Wages War on Truth', *The Guardian*, 18 August 2025, https://www.theguardian.com/us-news/2025/aug/18/trump-war-on-truth.

56. For example, by linking their performance reviews to the question whether they 'clearly and demonstrably' support Trump's agenda. J. Bendery, 'Trump's Performance Reviews Have a Troubling New Criteria', *HuffPost*, 27 October 2025, https://www.huffpost.com/entry/hhs-employees-trump-loyalty-performance-reviews_n_68ffa3b7e4b0ebfddfbaf88c.

57. D. J. Trump, 'Preventing Abuses of the Legal System and the Federal Court', The White House, 22 March 2025, https://www.whitehouse.gov/presidential-actions/2025/03/preventing-abuses-of-the-legal-system-and-the-federal-court/.

58. M. Smith and D. Simmons, 'Wisconsin Judge Indicted on Charges That She Helped Immigrant Evade Agents', *The New York Times*, 13 May 2025, https://www.nytimes.com/2025/05/13/us/milwaukee-judge-hannah-dugan-immigration.html.

59. 'Sharing the Facts About the Alien Enemies Act', States United Democracy Center, 17 March 2025, https://statesunited.org/resources/facts-about-alien-enemies-act/.

60. D. J. Trump, 'Countering Domestic Terrorism and Organized Political Violence', The White House, 25 September 2025, https://www.whitehouse.gov/presidential-actions/2025/09/countering-domestic-terrorism-and-organized-political-violence/.

61. 'Trump: "Enemy From Within" Should Be Handled by Military on Election Day', *WSJ News*, 14 October 2024, YouTube, https://www.youtube.com/watch?v=2YwVxLgWaTY.

62. Donald J. Trump on Truth Social, 22 March 2026, https://truthsocial.com/@realDonaldTrump/116272810363139207.

63. CBC News, 'Trump Decries "Enemy from Within", Threatens to Train Military in U.S. Cities', *The National*, 1 October 2025, https://www.youtube.com/watch?v=FJtS4wwsEiI.

64. A. Betts, 'Outrage after Trump Accuses Democrats of "Seditious Behavior, Punishable by Death"', *The Guardian*, 20 November 2025, https://www.theguardian.com/us-news/2025/nov/20/democrats-condemn-trump-military-video-post.

65. M. Haberman, C. Savage and J. Swan, 'Trump Suggests No Laws Are Broken If He's "Saving His Country"', *The New York Times*, 15 February 2025, https://www.nytimes.com/2025/02/15/us/politics/trump-saves-country-quote.html.

66. A study by the *Atlantic* shows the diversity of this mass movement. R. A. Pape and K. Ruby, 'The Capitol Rioters Aren't Like Other Extremists', *The Atlantic*, 2 February 2021, https://www.theatlantic.com/ideas/archive/2021/02/the-capitol-rioters-arent-like-other-extremists/617895/.

67. On January 6, 2026, the White published these lies on its website: 'January 6: A Date Which Will Live in Infamy', *The White House*, 6 January 2026, https://www.whitehouse.gov/j6/.

68. M. Dixon, 'Trump Delivers Fiery Post-Indictment Speech: "They're Coming after You"', NBC News, 11 June 2023, https://www.nbcnews.com/politics/donald-trump/trump-deliver-fiery-post-indictment-speech-georgia-rcna88561.

69. B. Stephens, 'Opinion | Trump Contrives His Stab-in-the-Back Myth', *The New York Times*, 24 November 2020, https://www.nytimes.com/2020/11/23/opinion/trump-biden-conspiracy-theory.html.

70. Since Trump's pardon, the Global Project Against Hate and Extremism has been following the Proud Boys' online channels, where members fantasize about how they can help Trump by assisting ICE with their mass deportations as a kind of subcontractor, and where they urge each other to report suspected illegal immigrants. R. Leingang, 'Proud Boys Leader Thanks Trump for January 6 Pardon and Vows Revenge', *The Guardian*, 24 January 2025, https://www.theguardian.com/us-news/2025/jan/24/trump-pardon-proud-boys-enrique-tarrio; A. Breland, 'Where Have the Proud Boys Gone?', *The Atlantic*, 5 August 2025, https://www.theatlantic.com/technology/archive/2025/08/proud-boys-militia-groups-trump-ice/683766/.

71. To do this, Trump set up a 'Weaponization Working Group' at the Department of Justice, led by Ed Martin, with the aim of investigating and potentially prosecuting the election officials who administered the 2020 election, prosecutors in Capitol riot

cases, and officials heavily involved with the Russia collusion investigation. As Martin told the *New York Post*, 'there may be no limit to the targets'. R. King, 'Trump's Weaponization Czar Ed Martin Hints at International Targets, Accepts That GOP Killed His Nomination: "It Worked out Great"', *New York Post*, 11 May 2025, https://nypost.com/2025/05/11/us-news/trumps-weaponization-czar-ed-martin-hints-at-international-targets-accepts-that-gop-killed-his-nomination-it-worked-out-great/. A study from NPR shows that Trump took revenge on more than a hundred opponents in the first hundred days of his second presidency. 'Trump Uses Government Powers to Target Perceived Enemies', *Consider This* from NPR, 29 April 2025, https://www.npr.org/2025/04/29/1247777260/trump-uses-government-powers-to-target-perceived-enemies.

72. Snyder, 'What Does It Mean That Donald Trump Is a Fascist?'

73. I. Ramírez and M. McCarthy, 'Republicans Embrace "Divine Intervention" for Trump's Near-Miss into Martyrdom', *Politico*, 14 July 2024, https://www.politico.com/news/2024/07/14/trump-shooting-republicans-god-intervention-00168108.

74. 'The Very American Roots of Trumpism', *The Ezra Klein Show*, 24 April 2024, https://www.youtube.com/watch?v=82tk31IHnoY.

75. E. Zerofsky, 'Is It Fascism? A Leading Historian Changes His Mind', *The New York Times Magazine*, 23 October 2024, https://www.nytimes.com/2024/10/23/magazine/robert-paxton-facism.html.

76. 'Yuval Noah Harari Believes AI Is the End of Human-Dominated History', *The Economist*, YouTube, 18 September 2023, https://www.youtube.com/shorts/vz3HKkVrJE4.

77. 'Yuval Noah Harari Believes AI Is the End of Human-Dominated History'.

78. See also: I. Trippenbach, 'The Heritage Foundation, MAGA's missionaries, sets its sights on Europe', *Le Monde*, 22 June 2025, https://www.lemonde.fr/en/m-le-mag/article/2025/06/22/the-heritage-foundation-sets-its-sights-on-europe_6742608_117.html.

79. 'Project 2025 Tracker', https://project2025.observer/en.

80. https://www.authoritarian-stack.info/.

81. P. Thiel, 'The Education of a Libertarian', *Cato Unbound*, 13 April 2009, https://www.cato-unbound.org/2009/04/13/peter-thiel/education-libertarian.

82. A. Kofman, 'Curtis Yarvin's Plot Against America', *The New Yorker*, 2 June 2025, https://www.newyorker.com/magazine/2025/06/09/curtis-yarvin-profile.

83. M. Andreessen, 'The Techno-Optimist Manifesto',

Andreessen Horowitz, 16 October 2023, https://a16z.com/the-techno-optimist-manifesto/.

84. For more information, see: 'The Authoritarian Stack', https://www.authoritarian-stack.info.

85. R. Ben-Ghiat, 'Trump's Authoritarian Innovations', Project Syndicate, 5 December 2025, https://www.project-syndicate.org/onpoint/how-trump-is-adding-to-the-traditional-authoritarian-playbook-by-ruth-ben-ghiat-2025-12.

86. For more information, see: 'The Authoritarian Stack'.

87. A. Rangappa, 'Making Sense of MAGA', *The Freedom Academy with Asha Rangappa*, Substack newsletter, 5 September 2025, https://asharangappa.substack.com/p/making-sense-of-maga.

88. Paxton, *The Anatomy of Fascism*.

89. S. Levitsky and D. Ziblatt, 'There Are Four Anti-Trump Pathways We Failed to Take. There Is a Fifth', *The New York Times*, 24 October 2024, https://www.nytimes.com/2024/10/24/opinion/democracy-defense-us-authoritarian.html.

90. S. Levitsky, L. Way and D. Ziblatt, 'How Will We Know When We Have Lost Our Democracy?', *The New York Times*, 8 May 2025, https://www.nytimes.com/2025/05/08/opinion/trump-authoritarianism-democracy.html, accessed 20 January 2026.

91. In 2025, the Federal Register counted 225 executive orders: https://www.federalregister.gov/presidential-documents/executive-orders/donald-trump/2025.

92. Alex Lemonides et al., 'Tracking the Lawsuits Against Trump's Agenda', *The New York Times*, 12 February 2025, https://www.nytimes.com/interactive/2025/us/trump-administration-lawsuits.html.

93. This was the dissenting opinion of Judge Ketanji Brown Jackson. She argued that the Court's decision gives the executive power room to violate the constitution against anyone who has not filed a lawsuit, who is therefore not a party. R. Abrams et al., 'Supreme Court Hands Trump Even More Power', *The Daily* podcast, *The New York Times*, 30 June 2025, https://www.nytimes.com/2025/06/30/podcasts/the-daily/trump-scotus-birthright.html.

94. M. Schwartz, E. Schartz and A. Parlapiano, 'Trump's "Superstar" Appellate Judges Have Voted 133 to 12 in His Favor', *The New York Times*, 11 January 2026, https://www.nytimes.com/2026/01/11/us/politics/trumps-appeals-court-judges.html.

95. E. Mystal, 'The Supreme Court's Shadowy Plan to Subvert Democracy', *The Nation*, 16 December 2025, https://www.thenation.com/article/society/supreme-court-shadow-docket-explainer/.

96. An investigation by the *New York Times* found that by far most of

them had no significant criminal record. Julie Turkewitz et al., 'Who Are the Venezuelan Deportees Sent to El Salvador?', *The New York Times*, 15 April 2025, https://www.nytimes.com/video/us/politics/100000010085123/who-are-the-venezuelan-deportees-sent-to-el-salvador.html.

97. Supreme Court of the United States, *Noem v. Abrego Garcia* No. 24A949, 604 U.S. ___, 10 April 2024, https://www.supremecourt.gov/opinions/24pdf/24a949_lkhn.pdf.

98. S. McCreesh and Z. Kanno-Youngs, 'Trump Would Not Concede "MS-13" Letters Were Digitally Added', *The New York Times*, 30 April 2025, https://www.nytimes.com/2025/04/30/us/trump-ms-13-tattoo-abrego-garcia.html.

99. Two prosecutors resigned in protest: one didn't want to go along with unsupported claims that Ábrego García was a gang member; the other indicated that 'the only job description I've ever known is to do to do the right thing, in the right way, for the right reasons'. N. Miroff, 'Trump's Running Tab in the Abrego Garcia Case', *The Atlantic*, 27 June 2025, https://www.theatlantic.com/politics/archive/2025/06/kilmar-abrego-garcia-tennessee-release/683357/.

100. A. Feuer, J. Ulloa and C. Cameron, 'Abrego Garcia Detained Again After Government Signaled It Would Re-Deport Him', *The New York Times*, 25 August 2025, https://www.nytimes.com/2025/08/25/us/politics/kilmar-abrego-garcia-arrested-ice-deportation.html.

101. *Kilmar Armando Abrego Garcia v. Kristi Noem et al.*, Civil Action No. 8:25-cv-02780-PX, 2025 WL citation number (D. Md. December 11, 2025), https://storage.courtlistener.com/recap/gov.uscourts.mdd.589189/gov.uscourts.mdd.589189.110.0_3.pdf.

102. A. Feuer, 'Abrego Garcia Is Released From ICE Detention After Judge's Order', *The New York Times*, 11 December 2025, https://www.nytimes.com/2025/12/11/us/politics/abrego-garcia-released.html.

103. B. Chappell, 'How ICE Grew to Be the Highest-Funded U.S. Law Enforcement Agency', *NPR*, 21 January 2026, https://www.npr.org/2026/01/21/nx-s1-5674887/ice-budget-funding-congress-trump.

104. 'Secretary Noem Unveils No Age Limit for Patriotic Americans to Join ICE Law Enforcement to Help Remove Worst of the Worst from U.S.', press release, U.S. Department of Homeland Security, 6 August 2025, https://www.dhs.gov/news/2025/08/06/secretary-noem-unveils-no-age-limit-patriotic-americans-join-ice-law-enforcement.

105. Check out the Department of Homeland Security's Instagram for countless examples: https://www.instagram.com/dhsgov/.

106. Homeland Security [@DHSgov], 'REMINDER. "To all ICE officers: You have federal immunity in the conduct of your duties. Anybody who lays a hand on you or tries to stop you or tries to obstruct you is committing a felony. You have immunity to perform your duties, and no one—no city official, no state official…" https://t.co/xoWDjOctLe', X, 13 January 2026, https://x.com/DHSgov/status/2011213308968538361.

107. The full names of the victims are listed in this article: M. Sing, C. Murphy Marcos and C. Simmonds, '2025 was ICE's deadliest year in two decades. Here are the 32 people who died in custody', *The Guardian*, https://www.theguardian.com/us-news/ng-interactive/2026/jan/04/ice-2025-deaths-timeline.

108. A. Baio, 'ICE Agents Ate at a Minnesota Mexican Restaurant before Arresting Staff', *The Independent*, 16 January 2026, https://www.independent.co.uk/news/world/americas/us-politics/ice-arrest-minnesota-mexican-restaurant-b2902000.html.

109. As five-year-old Liam Conejo Ramos returned from school, he was grabbed off the street by a heavily armed ICE agent and forced to knock on his own front door to get his family to come out. H. Yan and P. Alvarez, 'A Preschooler Was Taken Away by ICE, but Officials Say They Had No Choice. Here's What We Know', CNN, 23 January 2026, https://www.cnn.com/2026/01/23/us/liam-conejo-ramos-ice-wwk.

110. D. James and C. Wight, 'ICE arrests underdressed Hmong-American man inside his St. Paul home over mistaken identity, family says', CBS News, 20 January 2026, https://www.cbsnews.com/minnesota/news/ice-elderly-hmong-american-citizen-arrested-st-paul/.

111. R. A. Vargas, 'Renee Nicole Good Said "I'm Not Mad at You" before ICE Agent Shot Her, Video Shows', *The Guardian*, 9 January 2026, https://www.theguardian.com/us-news/2026/jan/09/ice-agent-minneapolis-bodycam-footage.

112. Associated Press, 'Man Shot and Killed by Federal Officers in Minnesota Was an ICU Nurse, His Parents Say', PBS News, 24 January 2026, https://www.pbs.org/newshour/nation/man-shot-and-killed-by-federal-officers-in-minnesota-was-an-icu-nurse-his-parents-say.

113. R. Sayre, interview on *All Things Considered*, NPR, 24 January 2026.

114. D. Smith, '"This Is What Fascism Looks like": Terror in Minneapolis Reminiscent of Civil War', *The Guardian*, 25 January 2026, https://www.theguardian.com/us-news/2026/jan/25/minneapolis-shooting-ice-trump-analysis.

115. B. Gibson, 'Trump Officials Stick "Terrorist" Label
     on Americans Killed by DHS', Axios, 25 January
     2026, https://www.axios.com/2026/01/25/
     trump-officials-stick-terrorist-label-on-americans-killed-by-dhs.
116. D. J. Trump, 'Countering Domestic Terrorism and
     Organized Political Violence', presidential memorandum,
     The White House, 25 September 2025, https://
     www.whitehouse.gov/presidential-actions/2025/09/
     countering-domestic-terrorism-and-organized-political-violence/.
117. Dept. of Homeland Security (@dhsgov), "'Blessed Are the
     Peacemakers, for They Shall Be Called Sons of God.' Matthew
     5:9"', Instagram post, 13 January 2026, https://www.instagram.
     com/dhsgov/reel/DTdjJu6CQ4U/.
118. A. Terkel and L. Hurley, 'Trump, Asked If He Has to "Uphold the
     Constitution," Says, "I Don't Know"', NBC News, 4 May 2025,
     https://www.nbcnews.com/politics/trump-administration/
     trump-asked-uphold-constitution-says-dont-know-rcna204580.
119. The goal is 'to test a once-fringe legal theory ['unitary executive
     theory'] which asserts that the president has unlimited power
     to control the actions of the four million people who make up
     the executive branch. If courts – specifically the Republican-
     appointed majority of the Supreme Court – uphold arguments
     based on the so-called "unitary executive theory," it would
     give Trump and subsequent presidents unprecedented power
     to remove and replace any federal employee and impose their
     will on every decision in every agency.' J. Knutson, 'What Is
     Unitary Executive Theory? How Is Trump Using It to Push His
     Agenda?', *Democracy Docket*, 20 February 2025, https://www.
     democracydocket.com/analysis/what-is-unitary-executive-theory-
     how-is-trump-using-it-to-push-his-agenda.
120. Rangappa elaborates on this in an episode of *The Ezra Klein Show*:
     'The Emergency Is Here', 17 April 2024, https://www.youtube.
     com/watch?v=JN1oBfg0fwI.
121. A. Parker and M. Scherer, '"I Run the Country and the World"', *The
     Atlantic*, 28 April 2025, https://www.theatlantic.com/magazine/
     archive/2025/06/trump-second-term-comeback/682573/.
122. M. Cullen, 'Trump Said His Global Power Was Limited Only by
     His "Own Morality"', *The New York Times*, 8 January 2026, https://
     www.nytimes.com/2026/01/08/briefing/trump-interview-oval-
     office-apple-ceo.html, accessed 27 February 2026.
123. ET Online, 'Davos 2026: Trump Calls Himself a "Dictator" at
     Davos, Rules out Force or Tariffs over Greenland', *Economic
     Times*, 22 January 2026, https://economictimes.indiatimes.com/

news/international/world-news/davos-2026-trump-calls-himself-a-dictator-at-davos-rules-out-force-or-tariffs-over-greenland/articleshow/127105878.cms.

124. The White House, 'January 6: A Date Which Will Live in Infamy', 6 January 2026, https://www.whitehouse.gov/j6/.

125. D. J. Trump, quoted on *All Things Considered*, NPR, 7 February 2026.

126. M. Elias, 'Trump's Call to Cancel Elections Must Be a Wake-up Call', Democracy Docket, 16 January 2026, https://www.democracydocket.com/opinion/trumps-call-to-cancel-elections-must-be-a-wake-up-call/.

127. B. Worthy, 'The 2026 Midterms: Trump Will Try and Steal the Midterms by Suppressing the Vote and Controlling the Narrative', *United States Politics and Policy*, 21 November 2025, https://blogs.lse.ac.uk/usappblog/2025/11/21/the-2026-midterms-trump-will-try-and-steal-the-midterms-by-suppressing-the-vote-and-controlling-the-narrative/.

128. N. McCann Ramirez, 'Trump Suggests Republicans Start Expelling Dems from Congress', *Rolling Stone*, 2 May 2025, https://www.rollingstone.com/politics/politics-news/trump-suggests-republicans-expelling-democrats-congress-1235330361/.

129. D. J. Trump, Truth Social post, 1 May 2025, https://truthsocial.com/@realDonaldTrump/posts/114436142904738936.

130. Carol Rose made this appeal on the podcast *Question Everything* with Brian Reed: '22. Rümeysa Öztürk Is Locked Up for an Op-Ed: An…', *Question Everything*, 1 May 2025, https://www.kcrw.com/shows/question-everything/stories/22-rumeysa-ozturk-is-locked-up-for-an-op-ed-an-urgent-summit-with-the-student-newspaper-that-published-it.

131. R. Igielnik and T. Pager, 'Trump's Approval Rating Dips as Views of His Handling of the Economy Sour', *The New York Times*, 5 December 2025, https://www.nytimes.com/2025/12/05/us/politics/trump-approval-rating.html.

132. E. Londoño and S. A. Rao, 'A Show of Defiance Across the Nation', *New York Times*, 28 March 2026, https://www.nytimes.com/2026/03/28/us/no-kings-protest-photos-videos.html.

133. S. Shepard and A. Daniller, 'Americans Broadly Disapprove of U.S. Military Action in Iran', *Pew Research*, March 2026. https://www.pewresearch.org/politics/2026/03/25/americans-broadly-disapprove-of-u-s-military-action-in-iran/.

134. M. S. Schmidt et al., 'In Trump's Second Term, Retribution Comes in Many Forms', *The New York Times*, 7 April 2025, https://www.nytimes.com/2025/04/07/us/politics/trump-biden-law-firms-revenge.html.

135. S. Hubler, 'Judge Says Trump's Use of Troops in L.A. Is Illegal', *The New York Times*, 2 September 2025, https://www.nytimes. com/2025/09/02/us/judge-ruling-trump-national-guard-los-angeles.html.

136. 'Trump News at a Glance: Gavin Newsom Declares "Democracy Is under Assault" in Blistering Attack on President', *The Guardian*, 11 June 2025, https://www.theguardian.com/us-news/2025/jun/11/trump-administration-news-updates-today.

137. A. Hartounian, 'The Story behind the Arrest of 87-Year-Old Veteran John Spitzberg at the Capitol', NPR, 20 June 2025, https://www.npr.org/2025/06/20/nx-s1-5438406/john-spitzberg-veteran-arrest-trump-parade.

138. A. Hassan, 'Elected Officials Who Have Been Detained in Protests', *The New York Times*, 17 June 2025, https://www.nytimes. com/2025/06/17/us/ice-arrests-elected-offcials.html.

139. 'In 2016, I declared: I am your voice… Today, I add: I am your warrior. I am your justice. And for those who have been wronged and betrayed: I am your retribution,' Donald Trump told the Conservative Political Action Conference on 4 March 2023.

140. Levitsky et al., 'How Will We Know When We Have Lost Our Democracy?'

3. Fascist patterns in Europe today

1. Finchelstein, *The Wannabe Fascists*.

2. J. Angelos & N. Nöstlinger, 'Trump Has Already Screwed over Germany's New Chancellor', *Politico*, 6 May 2025, https://www. politico.eu/article/donald-trump-germany-chancellor-afd-friedrich-merz/.

3. T. Joyner, 'Italy's Meloni Says "We Hope to Make the West Great Again" in Trump Meeting', BBC News, 17 April 2025, https:// www.bbc.com/news/live/cewgn4jnkd2t.

4. Giorgia Meloni, "#ItalianiAllEstero: In Italia Prove Generali Sostituzione Etnica, Perché Non Espatriano Incompetenti Che Ci Governano? ST https://T.Co/JJyRjlHNAE" ', X, 6 October 2016, https://x.com/GiorgiaMeloni/status/784044952124743682.

5. J. Horowitz, 'Giorgia Meloni May Lead Italy, and Europe Is Worried', *The New York Times*, 15 September 2022, https://www.nytimes. com/2022/09/15/world/europe/giorgia-meloni-italy-right.html.

6. Ben-Ghiat, 'Fascist Population Engineering'.

7. She criminalized surrogacy and recourse to surrogacy

anywhere in the world and rolled back 'co-motherhood' (two mothers registered as a child's parents). 'Italië verbiedt draagmoederschap zelfs in het buitenland, twijfels over haalbaarheid', NOS, 17 October 2024, https://nos.nl/artikel/2541058-italie-verbiedt-draagmoederschap-zelfs-in-het-buitenland-twijfels-over-haalbaarheid.

8.　G. Zandonini and M. Vermeulen, 'Cuffed, caged, cast-away. This is Europe's innovative solution for unwanted migrants', *De Correspondent*, 29 January 2026, https://decorrespondent.nl/16676/cuffed-caged-cast-away-this-is-europe-s-innovative-solution-for-unwanted-migrants/227673db-ddd2-02ec-2f5c-fbe266023128.

9.　J. Mommers, 'Hoe de rechtszaal het strijdtoneel werd van de vraag: wie heeft nu echt de macht in een democratie?', *De Correspondent*, 25 April 2025, https://decorrespondent.nl/16049/hoe-de-rechtszaal-het-strijdtoneel-werd-van-de-vraag-wie-heeft-nu-echt-de-macht-in-een-democratie/ae75d2a4-c1d0-02ee-070d-9460c0e10cd9.

10.　A. Chemin, 'National Preference: The Rassemblement National's Unconstitutional Key Promise', *Le Monde*, 30 June 2024, https://www.lemonde.fr/en/opinion/article/2024/06/30/national-preference-the-rassemblement-national-s-unconstitutional-key-promise_6676168_23.html.

11.　E. Ventura, 'France: Attempts to De-demonize the Radical Right – Charting the Radical Right's Influence on EU Foreign Policy', Carnegie Endowment for International Peace, 18 April 2024, https://carnegieendowment.org/russia-eurasia/research/2024/04/charting-the-radical-rights-influence-on-eu-foreign-policy.

12.　Find more info on the party website: RN – Rassemblement National, 'Législatives 2024' (n.d.), https://rassemblementnational.fr/legislatives-2024.

13.　D. de Groot, 'Hungary's Pride ban', European Parliamentary Research Service, 27 May 2025, https://www.europarl.europa.eu/RegData/etudes/BRIE/2025/775839/EPRS_BRI(2025)775839_EN.pdf.

14.　'Orbán Criticises EU and Vows to Reduce Foreign Influence in Hungary', Euronews, 15 March 2025, https://www.euronews.com/my-europe/2025/03/15/hungarys-russia-friendly-prime-minister-attacks-the-eu-in-nationalist-speech.

15.　According to research by *The PopuList*, together, far-right parties obtained 25 per cent of votes in all national elections, thereby overtaking the conservative and socialist democrat blocks. 'Hard-Right Parties Are Now Europe's Most Popular', *The Economist*, 28 February 2025,

https://www.economist.com/graphic-detail/2025/02/28/
hard-right-parties-are-now-europes-most-popular.

16. M. Nord, D. Altman, F. Tiago, A. Good God, and S. I. Lindberg,
    'Democracy Report 2026: Unraveling The Democratic Era?'
    University of Gothenburg, V-Dem Institute, https://www.v-dem.
    net/documents/75/V-Dem_Institute_Democracy_Report_2026_
    lowres.pdf.

17. Read the group manifesto on the Patriots' website: patriots.eu/
    manifesto.

18. Read more on the ESN Group website: esn-group.eu/
    what-we-stand-for.

19. M. Griera and M. Gros, 'EU Parliament Creates
    Official Body to Probe NGO Funding', *Politico*,
    19 June 2025, https://www.politico.eu/article/
    eu-parliament-creates-official-body-to-probe-ngo-funding/.

20. N. Nielsen, 'Why right-wing inquiry into Europe's NGOs was
    never about transparency', *euobserver*, 16 February 2026, https://
    euobserver.com/203164/why-rightwing-inquiry-into-europes-
    ngos-was-never-about-transparency/.

21. J. Mommers, 'Brussel zet de heggenschaar in eigen regels en
    richtlijnen. Blijft er genoeg over voor de groene revolutie?',
    De Correspondent, 30 June 2025, https://decorrespondent.
    nl/16203/brussel-zet-de-heggenschaar-in-eigen-regels-en-
    richtlijnen-blijft-er-genoeg-over-voor-de-groene-revolutie/
    eacc1cb8-1a85-0e7f-1bcb-02cd08e33130.

22. Y. Lacroix, 'Christendemocraten breken met "cordon sanitaire"
    – Politieke lijnen vervagen in het Europees Parlement',
    Brusselse Nieuwe, 25 October 2024, https://brusselsenieuwe.nl/
    christendemocraten-breken-met-cordon-sanitaire-politieke-lijnen-
    vervagen-in-het-europees-parlement/.

23. M. Goslinga, 'Minder regels? Regelgeving is juist Europa's
    geheime wapen', *De Correspondent*, 14 November
    2025, https://decorrespondent.nl/16542/minder-
    regels-regelgeving-is-juist-europa-s-geheime-wapen/
    e5eff25c-1dfb-0b66-079d-69f6c711d5f5.

24. European Parliament, 'Migration: the Civil Liberties Committee
    adopts a reform of EU return rules', 9 March 2026, https://www.
    europarl.europa.eu/news/en/press-room/20260309IPR37702/
    migration-the-civil-liberties-committee-adopts-a-reform-of-eu-
    return-rules.

25. J. Rankin and A. Giuffrida, 'Von Der Leyen to Ask EU Leaders
    to Explore Using "Return Hubs" for Migrants' *The Guardian*, 15
    October 2024, https://www.theguardian.com/world/2024/oct/15/

ursual-von-der-leyen-to-ask-eu-leaders-to-explore-using-return-hubs-for-migrants.

26. G. Katawazi, 'Weinig zetels, veel tumult: hoe radicaal-rechts de Europese politiek steeds meer naar zijn hand zet', *De Correspondent*, 2 April 2025, https://decorrespondent.nl/16002/weinig-zetels-veel-tumult-hoe-radicaal-rechts-de-europese-politiek-steeds-meer-naar-zijn-hand-zet/a582c8fa-19b1-082f-0497-d43f7c458ab3.

27. Paxton, *The Anatomy of Fascism*.

28. This research mapped 3,000 speakers from 1,800 organizations at 302 events in 35 countries from 2000 to 2024. 'Mapping The Far Right: The Movement's Conferences Illuminates Its Growing Transnational Networks', *Global Project Against Hate and Extremism*, 5 December 2024, https://globalextremism.org/reports/mapping-the-far-right-the-movements-conferences-illuminate-its-growing-transnational-networks/.

29. M. Losonczi, 'Center for Fundamental Rights Announces Wokebusters Task Force', *Hungarian Conservative*, 30 July 2024, https://www.hungarianconservative.com/articles/current/wokebusters_center-for-fundamental-rights_gavin-wax/.

30. Read more on the CPAC Hungary website: https://www.cpachungary.com/en/.

31. Interview with Jelle Postma, 9 July 2025.

32. L. Nordstrom, 'In the Name of the Family: Yes, Europe Could Be Headed for a "Project 2025" Too', France 24, 21 March 2025, https://www.france24.com/en/europe/20250321-in-the-name-of-the-family-yes-europe-could-be-headed-project-2025-too-lgbtq-trump-far-right-heritage-foundation.

33. T. Greven, *The Radical Right in Europe: Transnational Networks*, 2024, http://collections.fes.de/publikationen/1572530.

34. See also this similar discussion: N. Datta, *Restoring the Natural Order: The Religious Extremists' Vision to Mobilize European Societies Against Human Rights on Sexuality and Reproduction*, European Parliamentary Forum on Population & Development, Brussels, April 2018, https://www.epfweb.org/sites/default/files/2020-05/rtno_epf_book_lores.pdf.

35. See the Ordo Iuris website: https://ordoiuris.pl/en/legal-interventions/. It states, for example, that its aim is to 'exert active and professional influence on judicial and administrative… cases involving… the freedoms of conscience and speech of those who are socially excluded because of their value system'. Another example can be found on the ADF International website: http://adfinternational.org/training.

36. A. Coakley, 'The Mysterious Lawyers Trying to Create Europe's Most Ultra-Conservative State', *VICE*, 28 September 2021, https://www.vice.com/en/article/ordo-iuris-the-mysterious-lawyers-trying-to-create-europes-most-ultra-conservative-state/.

37. Alliance Defending Freedom, 'What You May Not Know: How ADF Helped Overturn Roe v. Wade', ADF Legal, 10 January 2024, https://adflegal.org/article/what-you-may-not-know-how-adf-helped-overturn-roe-v-wade/.

38. O. Bault et al, *Advocacy in International Institutions: A Guide for Non-Governmental Organizations That Want to Engage in the Protection of Human Rights in the International Arena*, Academic Publishing House of the Ordo Iuris Institute for Legal Culture, Warsaw, 2025, https://ordoiuris.pl/wp-content/uploads/2025/05/advocacy_in_international_institutions_digital.pdf.

39. Ordo Iuris website: 'Ordo Iuris joins pro-life coalition at 69th session of UN Commission on the Status of Women', 18 March 2025, https://ordoiuris.pl/en/press-newsdesk/ordo-iuris-joins-pro-life-coalition-at-69th-session-of-un-commission-on-status-of-women.

40. Interview with Federico Finchelstein on 28 December 2025.

41. E. Bubola, 'Far-Right Leaders Rally in Spain to "Make Europe Great Again"', *The New York Times*, 8 February 2025, https://www.nytimes.com/2025/02/08/world/europe/far-right-spain-rally.html.

42. Interview with Federico Finchelstein on 28 December 2025.

43. P. Bernard et al., 'Behind the Words of JD Vance's Historic Munich Speech', *Le Monde*, 21 February 2025, https://www.lemonde.fr/en/opinion/article/2025/02/21/behind-the-words-of-jd-vance-s-historic-munich-speech_6738424_23.html.

44. S. Samson, 'The Need for Civilizational Allies in Europe', U.S. Department of State, 27 May 2025, https://statedept.substack.com/p/the-need-for-civilizational-allies-in-europe.

45. Hitler, *Mein Kampf.*

46. The White House, *National Security Strategy of the United States of America.*

47. US Department of State, 'Announcement of Actions to Combat the Global Censorship-Industrial Complex', press release, 23 December 2025, https://www.state.gov/releases/office-of-the-spokesperson/2025/12/announcement-of-actions-to-combat-the-global-censorship-industrial-complex/.

48. A. Hernández-Morales, 'US Sanctions Former EU Commissioner and Four Europeans over Efforts to Curb Online Hate Speech', *Politico*, 24 December 2025, https://www.politico.eu/article/us-sanctions-former-eu-commissioner-thierry-breton-for-curbing-online-hate-speech/.

49. Interview with Catherine de Vries on 29 March 2026.

50. The Heritage Foundation, *Mandate for Leadership: The Conservative Promise*, Project 2025, Presidential Transition Project, Washington, DC, April 2023, https://static.heritage.org/project2025/2025_MandateForLeadership_FULL.pdf.

51. 'We are very concerned about the West,' Roberts said in an interview with the French newspaper *Le Monde*. 'I don't care what the radical left says about me… I just want to beat them. In every election for the rest of my life.' I. Trippenbach 'The Heritage Foundation, MAGA's Missionaries, Sets Its Sights on Europe', *Le Monde*, 22 June 2025, https://www.lemonde.fr/en/m-le-mag/article/2025/06/22/the-heritage-foundation-sets-its-sights-on-europe_6742608_117.html.

52. R. Ballester et al., *The Great Reset: Restoring Member State Sovereignty in the European Union: A Two Scenario Proposal Through Institutional Reform for a New EU from Mathias Corvinus Collegium and Ordo Iuris Institute*, Academic Publishing House of the Ordo Iuris Institute for Legal Culture and Mathias Corvinus Collegium, Warsaw and Budapest, 2025, https://legrandcontinent.eu/fr/wp-content/uploads/sites/2/2025/03/The_Great_Reset_Restoring_Member_State_Sovereignty_0-2.pdf.

53. 'What Is the Great Reset – and How Did It Get Hijacked by Conspiracy Theories?', BBC News, 24 June 2021, https://www.bbc.com/news/blogs-trending-57532368.

54. S. Panyi, 'Renaming the EU, Dismantling the Commission: Polish, Hungarian Illiberals Seek U.S. Backing', VSquare.Org, 10 March 2025, https://vsquare.org/heritage-foundation-mcc-ordo-iuris-russia-european-union-european-court-of-justice/.

55. R. Ballester and J. Kwasniewski, 'Souveraineté : "À quand un "great reset" de l'Union européenne?"' *Le Figaro*, 7 November 2025, https://www.lefigaro.fr/vox/monde/souverainete-a-quand-un-great-reset-de-l-union-europeenne-20251107.

56. Quote by Ordo Iuris spokesperson to the Spanish newspaper *El País*. Á. Munárriz, 'The Great Reset: The Far Right's Detailed Plan to Dismantle the EU', *El País*, 14 June 2025, https://english.elpais.com/international/2025-06-14/the-great-reset-the-far-rights-detailed-plan-to-dismantle-the-eu.html.

57. A. Roston and C. Brown, '"They're Trying to Get Rich off It": US Contractors Vie to Rebuild Gaza, with "Alligator Alcatraz" Team in the Lead', *The Guardian*, 14 December 2025, https://www.theguardian.com/us-news/2025/dec/14/gaza-rebuild-us-contractors.

58. D. Gritten, 'US unveils plans for "New Gaza" with skyscrapers',

BBC News, 22 January 2026, https://www.bbc.com/news/articles/cy7mmpljze7o.

59. A. Loewenstein, *The Palestine Laboratory: How Israel Exports the Technology of Occupation around the World*, Verso Books, 2023.

60. D. Estrin, 'After two years of war, Israeli weapons makers showcase their new tech', *All Things Considered*, NPR, 3 December 2025, https://www.npr.org/2025/12/03/nx-s1-5628404/after-two-years-of-war-israeli-weapons-makers-showcase-their-new-tech.

61. A. Goodfriend, 'U.S. Companies Honed Their Surveillance Tech in Israel. Now It's Coming Home', *The Intercept*, 30 April 2025, https://theintercept.com/2025/04/30/israel-palestine-us-ai-surveillance-state/.

62. In 2024, the International Court of Justice ruled that Israel's occupation of the Palestinian territories is unlawful, see 'Legal Consequences arising from the Policies and Practices of Israel in the Occupied Palestinian Territory, including East Jerusalem', International Court of Justice, 19 July 2024, https://www.icj-cij.org/case/131.

63. Israel controls the entire occupied Palestinian territory, including Gaza. An occupying power does not have the right to defend itself against a threat from the area it controls. The International Court of Justice already ruled on this in its opinion on Israel's construction of a wall running for kilometres on Palestinian territory.

64. Global Centre for the Responsibility to Protect, 'Defining the Four Mass Atrocity Crimes', Global R2P, 15 August 2018, https://www.globalr2p.org/publications/defining-the-four-mass-atrocity-crimes/.

65. L. Admiraal and M. Kerres, 'Sigrid Kaag over haar werk voor de VN in Gaza: "Als de dood een verlossing wordt, zijn we heel erg van het pad af",' *NRC*, 20 June 2025, https://www.nrc.nl/nieuws/2025/06/20/sigrid-kaag-over-haar-werk-voor-de-vn-in-gaza-als-de-dood-een-verlossing-wordt-zijn-we-heel-erg-van-het-pad-af-a4897677/.

66. See https://www.icj-cij.org/node/203447.

67. E. Derakhshan, 'Waarom is Netanyahu nog niet gearresteerd? (En vijf andere vragen over de vervolging van Israëls gruweldaden)', *De Correspondent*, 27 January 2025, https://decorrespondent.nl/15841/waarom-is-netanyahu-nog-niet-gearresteerd-en-vijf-andere-vragen-over-de-vervolging-van-israels-gruweldaden/76f6ecc7-e866-08dd-24d0-3f5cde9f046b.

68. On 31 August 2025, the International Association of Genocide Scholars (IAGS), an association of 500 academics and legal experts, adopted a resolution stating that 'Israel's policies and

actions in Gaza meet the legal definition of genocide in Article II of the United Nations Convention for the Prevention and Punishment of the Crime of Genocide (1948)'. See: See: https://genocidescholars.org/wp-content/uploads/2025/08/IAGS-Resolution-on-Gaza-FINAL.pdf.

69. UN Human Rights Council, *Legal Analysis of the Conduct of Israel in Gaza Pursuant to the Convention on the Prevention and Punishment of the Crime of Genocide*, Conference Room Paper A/HRC/60/CRP.3, Sixtieth Session, 16 September 2025, https://www.ohchr.org/sites/default/files/documents/hrbodies/hrcouncil/sessions-regular/session60/advance-version/a-hrc-60-crp-3.pdf.

70. R. Smits, 'Nederland wil oorlogsmisdrijven voorkomen, maar handelen ho maar', *De Correspondent*, 15 February 2024, https://decorrespondent.nl/15133/nederland-wil-oorlogsmisdrijven-voorkomen-maar-handelen-ho-maar/8ec4727e-6b92-0ae0-2a8e-3391b53033a5.

71. Tweede Kamer der Staten-Generaal, *Motie van het lid Kuik c.s. over de kwalificatie van wreedheden door IS als genocide en misdaden tegen de menselijkheid*, Kamerstuk 29754-610, 1 July 2021, https://www.tweedekamer.nl/downloads/document?id=2021D26770.

72. Admiraal and Kerres, 'Sigrid Kaag over haar werk voor de VN in Gaza'.

73. J. Stegeman, 'Bevrijdingstheologie: christendom kan ook antikapitalistisch, antikoloniaal en antizionistisch zijn', *Jacobin Nederland*, 24 August 2025, https://jacobin.nl/bevrijdingstheologie-christendom-kan-ook-antikapitalistisch-antikoloniaal-en-antizionistisch-zijn/.

74. Office of the High Commissioner for Human Rights (OHCHR), 'Forever-Occupation, genocide, and profit: Special Rapporteur's report exposes corporate forces behind destruction of Palestine', press release, 3 July 2025, https://www.ohchr.org/en/press-releases/2025/07/forever-occupation-genocide-and-profit-special-rapporteurs-report-exposes, accessed 27 February 2026.

75. G. Wilders, 'Geert Wilders for Breitbart: Why Western Patriots Should Support Israel', Breitbart, 3 October 2024, https://www.breitbart.com/europe/2024/10/03/geert-wilders-for-breitbart-why-european-patriots-should-support-israel/.

76. The Heritage Foundation, 'Project Esther: A National Strategy to Combat Antisemitism', October 2024, https://www.heritage.org/progressivism/report/project-esther-national-strategy-combat-antisemitism.

77. K. J. M. Baker, 'Inside the Heritage Foundation's Plan to Crush the U.S. Palestinian Movement', *The New York Times*, 18 May

2025, https://www.nytimes.com/2025/05/18/us/project-esther-heritage-foundation-palestine.html.

78. Poll by J. Arm and M. Knee, 'The New GOP: Survey Analysis of Americans Overall, Today's Republican Coalition, and the Minorities of MAGA', Manhattan Institute, 1 December 2025, https://manhattan.institute/article/the-new-gop-survey-analysis-of-americans-overall-todays-republican-coalition-and-the-minorities-of-maga.

79. K. J. M. Baker et al, 'Video: Inside a Plan to Shut Down Pro-Palestinian Activism', *The New York Times*, 18 May 2025, https://www.nytimes.com/video/us/politics/100000010154898/inside-a-plan-to-shut-down-pro-palestinian-activism.html.

80. F. Regalado et al, 'U.S. Imposes Sanctions on U.N. Expert Who Has Denounced Israel Over Gaza War', *The New York Times*, 10 July 2025, https://www.nytimes.com/2025/07/10/us/politics/gaza-francesca-albanese-sanctions.html. Due to her statements on Israel's war crimes, UN rapporteur Francesca Albanese was not welcome at the Dutch parliament either. This was the first time access for a UN rapporteur had ever been refused. 'She hates Jews and Israel,' said PVV member of parliament Raymond de Roon.

81. The UN Human Rights Office of the High Commissioner, 'USA: UN expert demands withdrawal of sanctions against ICC judges and prosecutors, calls for repeal of executive order', 26 January 2026 https://www.ohchr.org/en/press-releases/2026/01/usa-un-expert-demands-withdrawal-sanctions-against-icc-judges-and.

82. 'Israël wil publieke opinie veranderen en steekt tientallen miljoenen extra in propaganda', NOS, 23 March 2025, https://nos.nl/collectie/13959/artikel/2560806-israel-wil-publieke-opinie-veranderen-en-steekt-tientallen-miljoenen-extra-in-propaganda.

83. The Dutch National Coordinator for Security and Counterterrorism (NCTV) therefore classifies Israel as a threat to Dutch security. See: https://www.rijksoverheid.nl/documenten/rapporten/2025/07/17/tk-bijlage-dbsa-2025-opgemaakte-versie.

84. After Israel accused, without any evidence, twelve staff members of United Nations Relief and Works Agency for Palestine Refugees (UNRWA) of terrorism, nineteen countries suspended their contribution to the aid organization in 2024, thereby supporting Israel's announced campaign to cut off the Gazans' last lifeline. R. Smits, 'De hulp in Gaza staat op instorten – mede dankzij Nederland', *De Correspondent*, 5 March 2024, https://decorrespondent.nl/15173/de-hulp-in-gaza-staat-op-instorten-mede-dankzij-nederland/61b92b4b-4666-00e5-3fa6-ac66e7975f83.

85. R. Verkerk, 'Israël valt journalisten doelgericht aan (en het
    Westen moet dat niet langer pikken)', *De Correspondent*,
    2 December 2024, https://decorrespondent.nl/15741/
    israel-valt-journalisten-doelgericht-aan-en-het-westen-moet-dat-
    niet-langer-pikken/1fb941be-9ae2-0cf9-2cb3-1650ac4790e5.
86. OHCHR, 'UN Experts Urge United Kingdom Not to Misuse
    Terrorism Laws against Protest Group Palestine Action',
    press release, 1 July 2025, https://www.ohchr.org/en/
    press-releases/2025/07/un-experts-urge-united-kingdom-not-
    misuse-terrorism-laws-against-protest.
87. Amnesty International UK, 'UK: Banning Palestine Action "a
    Disturbing Legal Overreach" by UK Government, Amnesty
    International UK Chief Executive Warns', press release, 2 July
    2025, https://www.amnesty.org.uk/latest/uk-banning-palestine-
    action-disturbing-legal-overreach-uk-government-amnesty/.
88. S. Gecsoyler and D. Gayle, 'Met Police Arrest Activists Holding
    Signs Referring to Palestine Action', *The Guardian*, 5 July
    2025, https://www.theguardian.com/uk-news/2025/jul/05/
    palestine-action-activists-arrested-london-gandhi-statue.
89. 'Palestine Action Protests: Arrests – Hansard – UK Parliament',
    23 July 2025, https://hansard.parliament.uk/lords/2025-07-
    23/debates/EE9FE2BF-425F-4A14-AF00-71B2F54069ED/
    PalestineActionProtestsArrests. And later: '200 arrestaties bij
    demonstraties in Londen', NOS, 9 August 2025, 'https://nos.nl/
    collectie/13959/liveblog/2577501-al-jazeera-doden-van-journalist-
    is-aanval-op-persvrijheid-australie-gaat-palestina-erkennen.
90. H. Siddique, 'UK Palestine Action ban ruled unlawful, in
    humiliating blow for ministers', *The Guardian*, 13 February
    2026, https://www.theguardian.com/uk-news/2026/feb/13/
    uk-ban-palestine-action-unlawful-high-court-judges-rule.
91. See: https://www.rijksoverheid.nl/actueel/nieuws/2025/06/20/
    ministerraad-stemt-in-met-wetsvoorstel-om-verheerlijken-van-
    terrorisme-strafbaar-te-stellen.
92. I. Dirksen and H. Kuloglu, 'Waarom de watermeloen het
    symbool van Palestijns verzet is', RTL Nieuws, 19 September
    2024, https://www.rtl.nl/nieuws/buitenland/artikel/5471593/
    gaza-palestijnse-gebieden-westbank-watermeloen-verzet.
93. G. Wilders [@geertwilderspvv], 'Vandaag 'n demo in DHaag
    tegen Israël + voor Hamas. Duizenden verwarde mensen
    trekken een rode lijn. Ik trek ook een rode lijn. Tegen terreur en
    het uithongeren vd eigen bevolking door #Hamas en voor het
    maximaal vernietigen van hun moorddadige infrastructuur. En
    voor #Israël. https://t.co/UhINheF7wh', X, 18 May 2025, https://x.

com/geertwilderspvv/status/1924050976333279601.

94. G. Wilders [@geertwilderspvv], 'Ze hebben veel te lang het antisemitisme en de jodenhaat van extreem links en radicale allochtonen toegestaan in Nederland en collectief de andere kant op gekeken. Een burgemeester die toestaat dat antisemitische tuig mag demonstreren op de dag van de opening van het', X, 8 October 2024, https://x.com/geertwilderspvv/status/1843653931555078210.

95. N. Klein, 'Surrealism Against Fascism', *Equator*, 26 November 2025, https://www.equator.org/articles/surrealism-against-fascism.

96. R. Fausset and K. Bensinger, 'Turning Point's Annual Gathering Turns Into a Gripefest', *The New York Times*, 21 December 2025, https://www.nytimes.com/2025/12/20/us/politics/turning-points-americafest-ben-shapiro.html.

97. A. Lotz, 'Trump Defends Tucker Carlson as Nick Fuentes Interview Divides MAGA World', Axios, 17 November 2025, https://www.axios.com/2025/11/17/trump-tucker-carlson-nick-fuentes-interview.

98. R. Verkerk, 'Om haat te bestrijden, moet je de extremist in jezelf onder ogen zien', *De Correspondent*, 17 December 2025, https://decorrespondent.nl/16612/om-haat-te-bestrijden-moet-je-de-extremist-in-jezelf-onder-ogen-zien/6e2673c4-44f5-05e5-264f-0992a67d9d14.

99. W. Churchill, United States of Europe Speech, 19 September 1946 https://winstonchurchill.org/resources/speeches/1946-1963-elder-statesman/united-states-of-europe/.

100. A. Applebaum, *Autocracy, Inc.: The Dictators Who Want to Run the World*, London: Allen Lane/Penguin Books Ltd, 2024.

101. D. D. Kirkpatrick, 'How Much Is Trump Profiting Off the Presidency?', *The New Yorker*, 11 August 2025, https://www.newyorker.com/magazine/2025/08/18/the-number.

102. M. Dunai, 'How Europe's Taxpayers Will Bankroll Viktor Orban's Friends and Family', Reuters, 15 March 2018, http://www.reuters.com/investigates/special-report/hungary-orban-balaton/.

103. Z. Palomo, 'Trump Brags That Friend Charles Schwab Made $2bn from Stock Market Chaos', *Independent*, 11 April 2025, https://www.independent.co.uk/tv/news/trump-charles-schwab-stock-market-tariffs-nascar-b2731568.html.

104. M. Goslinga, 'Minder regels? Regelgeving is juist Europa's geheime wapen', *De Correspondent*, 14 November 2025, https://decorrespondent.nl/16542/minder-regels-regelgeving-is-juist-europa-s-geheime-wapen/e5eff25c-1dfb-0b66-079d-69f6c711d5f5.

105. T. Bateman, 'US Says Countries with DEI Policies as Infringing Human Rights', BBC News, 21 November 2025, https://www.bbc.com/news/articles/cx24200d7y9o.

106. 'Breaches of EU Values: How the EU Can Act (Infographic)', European Parliament, 27 February 2018, https://www.europarl.europa.eu/topics/en/article/20180222STO98434/breaches-of-eu-values-how-the-eu-can-act-infographic.

107. Further information about the Court of Human Rights is available at: https://www.echr.coe.int.

108. Govt of Italy et al, 'Open Letter', 22 May 2025, https://www.governo.it/sites/governo.it/files/Lettera_aperta_22052025.pdf.

4. A case study: the fascist playbook in the Netherlands

1. Article 1 of the Dutch Constitution, https://open.overheid.nl/documenten/ronl-faa96875fef77af167a9133bd3625c0e9b45fa89/pdf.

2. J. Henley, '"Vicious Cycle": How Far-Right Parties across Europe Are Cannibalising the Centre Right', *The Guardian*, 1 February 2025, https://www.theguardian.com/world/2025/feb/01/vicious-cycle-far-right-parties-across-europe-are-inspiring-imitators.

3. On party discipline, see: Renee van Hest e.a., 'Het bastion van de PVV-fractie onder de loep', NOS, 19 February 2025, https://nos.nl/nieuwsuur/artikel/2556510-het-bastion-van-de-pvv-fractie-onder-de-loep.

4. C. de Vries, 'Nato's Mark Rutte Era', *New Statesman*, 26 June 2024, https://www.newstatesman.com/international-content/2024/06/natos-mark-rutte-era.

5. From an interview on 2 July 2025 with politics professor and president of the Institute for European Policymaking at the Bocconi University, Milan, Catherine de Vries.

6. A. Estrada, 'Door het te hebben over "migranten" in plaats van "moslims" kreeg Geert Wilders het hele parlement mee', *De Correspondent*, 23 May 2025, https://decorrespondent.nl/16114/door-het-te-hebben-over-migranten-in-plaats-van-moslims-kreeg-geert-wilders-het-hele-parlement-mee/7b342614-8fcf-0028-0183-615f7ea57cda.

7. See also Jesse Frederik on this normalization. 'What is striking in the national voter survey is that Dutch people seem to have somewhat forgotten "less, less, less". On integration, they rated the PVV one whole point (on a scale of 1 to 7) less extreme than a year ago. The Geert Milders act did a

great job in that regard.' J. Frederik, 'Waarom links steeds verkiezingen verliest (en nee, niet omdat de kiezer links niet begrijpt)', *De Correspondent*, 27 November 2024, https://decorrespondent.nl/15683/waarom-links-steeds-verkiezingen-verliest-en-nee-niet-omdat-de-kiezer-links-niet-begrijpt/c69ae80a-340a-01c8-287d-24c407aa70db.

8. Y. Eski, 'Academisch verzet kan ontwakend polderfascisme in de kiem smoren', *ScienceGuide*, 25 September 2024. See also J. Boersema, 'Wie bevrijdt 4 mei van de polderfascisten?', *One World*, 2 May 2025 https://www.oneworld.nl/mensenrechten/wie-bevrijdt-4-mei-van-de-polderfascisten/.

9. R. van de Griend, 'Denkbeelden Baudet worden steeds radicaler, signaleren vriend en vijand', *de Volkskrant*, 18 October 2022, https://www.volkskrant.nl/nieuws-achtergrond/denkbeelden-baudet-worden-steeds-radicaler-signaleren-vriend-en-vijand~babae587/.

10. J. Reygaert, 'Geen premier Geert Wilders in Nederland? Rechts-radicale politicus wil post opgeven voor rechtse meerderheid', *VRT NWS*, 13 March 2024, https://www.vrt.be/vrtnws/nl/2024/03/13/wilders-laat-premierschap-in-nederland-gaan-in-ruil-voor-steun-v/.

11. Interview with Federico Finchelstein on 28 December 2025.

12. You can find it on the Nieuwscheckers website if you search for 'Wilders': nieuwscheckers.nl.

13. AI-Filmpje van Wilders over 'Islamitisch Nederland' in 2050 Wakkert Angst Aan, WNL, 18 July 2025, https://www.youtube.com/watch?v=6J4l_aALzC0.

14. Partij voor deVrijheid *TK Verkiezingsprogramma 2025: Dit is úw land*, August 2025, https://www.pvv.nl/images/2025/PVV_Programma_Digi_2025.pdf.

15. G. Wilders on X: "De Israël-Haat Spat Weer van Het Scherm van Het NOS-Journaal Af. Dat Zijn Geen Journalisten Maar Enge Linkse Activisten." X, 5 August 2025, https://x.com/geertwilderspvv/status/1952806437597724949.

16. R. van Hest e.a., 'Strategisch en gesloten: zo stuurt Geert Wilders de PVV-fractie aan', NOS, 19 February 2025, https://nos.nl/nieuwsuur/artikel/2556509-strategisch-en-gesloten-zo-stuurt-geert-wilders-de-pvv-fractie-aan.

17. W. van Loon and Bas Haan, 'De X-factor van Geert Wilders: een analyse van 21.000 tweets van de PVV-leider', *NRC*, 17 June 2025, https://www.nrc.nl/nieuws/2025/06/17/de-x-factor-van-geert-wilders-een-analyse-van-21-000-tweets-van-de-pvv-leider-a4897192.

18. See the PVV 2023 election programme: https://www.pvv.nl/
images/2023/PVV-Verkiezingsprogramma-2023.pdf. See also T.
Beemsterboer, 'NPO en de omroepen vragen om terugdraaien
van geplande bezuinigingen', *NRC*, 6 June 2025, https://www.
nrc.nl/nieuws/2025/06/06/npo-en-de-omroepen-vragen-om-
terugdraaien-van-geplande-bezuinigingen-a4896146.

19. See the PVV 2025 election programme.

20. E. Demkes, 'Wat beweert Wilders? "Een islamitische invasie van
testosteron-bommen met baarden"', *OneWorld*, 6 October 2015,
https://www.oneworld.nl/mensenrechten/wat-beweert-wilders-
een-islamitische-invasie-van-testosteron-bommen-met-baarden/.

21. Rodaportal, '"CLOSE THE BORDERS!" – Geert Wilders'
CPAC Speech STUNS Europe | TRUTH About ISLAM &
IMMIGRATION', YouTube, 14 June 2025, https://www.youtube.
com/watch?v=S_OgIEbDRaw.

22. G. Wilders, General Financial Debate on Budget Memorandum
in the Dutch parliament, The Hague, 17 September 2025, https://
www.tweedekamer.nl/kamerstukken/plenaire_verslagen/
detail/2025-2026/2.

23. J. de Groot, 'Moslimorganisaties doen aangifte tegen Wilders
om "nazibeeldtaal"' *NRC*, 11 August 2025, https://www.nrc.nl/
nieuws/2025/08/11/moslimorganisaties-doen-aangifte-tegen-
wilders-om-nazibeeldtaal-a4902678.

24. A. Estrada, 'Door het te hebben over "migranten" in plaats van
"moslims" kreeg Geert Wilders het hele parlement mee', *De
Correspondent*, 23 May 2025, https://decorrespondent.nl/16114/
door-het-te-hebben-over-migranten-in-plaats-van-moslims-kreeg-
geert-wilders-het-hele-parlement-mee/7b342614-8fcf-0028-0183-
615f7ea57cda.

25. PVV Election Programme 'Dit is uw land!' (2025).

26. M. Peeperkorn, 'De anti-Europese Patriotten willen de EU van
binnenuit slopen, maar stuiten op een muur van tegenstand',
de Volkskrant, 9 July 2024, https://www.volkskrant.nl/politiek/
de-anti-europese-patriotten-willen-de-eu-van-binnenuit-slopen-
maar-stuiten-op-een-muur-van-tegenstand~b721f397/.

27. G. Oost and H. Schiffers, 'Kabinet wil snoeien in
ontwikkelingshulp: "Als iets wordt wegbezuinigd, is de kans heel
klein dat het terugkomt"', *NRC*, 11 August 2025.

28. X post by Geert Wilders, 20 February 2025.

29. Development aid is being cut by €500 million. The focus is now
on the Netherlands and how it can benefit from investment in
developing countries. 'Alleen nog ontwikkelingshulp als Nederland
er baat bij heeft: waarom?', RTL Nieuws, 20 February 2025.

30. See the PVV 2025 election programme.
31. Rodaportal, 'CLOSE THE BORDERS!'
32. See the PVV 2025 election programme.
33. See the PVV 2025 election programme.
34. G. Wilders, 'Natuurwet. Stikstofwet. Klimaatwet. De Links-Liberale Gekkies Maken Ons Land En Onze Boeren Helemaal Kapot. https://T.Co/cZOme4ze5G', X, 24 May 2023, https://x.com/geertwilderspvv/status/1661243701056913410.
35. G. Wilders, 'De Stikstofplannen Moeten Helemaal van Tafel. Niet Stikstof Maar de Boerenhaat van Dit Kabinet Maakt Nederland Kapot. Ze Willen Boeren Wegpesten En Op Hun Grond Zullen Dadelijk Wel Nieuwe Assielzoekerscentra Worden Gebouwd. Waanzin. Laat de Boeren #boeren! #boerenprotest https://T.Co/4UuLDfzh6e', X, 22 June 2022, https://x.com/geertwilderspvv/status/1539487046439419905.
36. J. Veerbeek and C. van de Ven, 'Wil de echte elite opstaan?', *De Groene Amsterdammer*, 4 December 2024.
37. See the PVV 2025 election programme.
38. J. Peters, 'Wilders doet aangifte tegen officieren van justitie om politieke inmenging', nu.nl, 9 September 2019.
39. 'Hongarije krijgt omstreden grondwet', NOS, 18 April 2011.
40. L. van de Ven, 'Achahbar hekelt "polariserende omgangsvormen" in vertrekbrief', *NRC*, 15 November 2024.
41. 'Kabinet en coalitie weer op één lijn over Oekraïne-steun: "Kou is uit de lucht"', *AD*, 13 March 2025.
42. Gessen, *Surviving Autocracy*.
43. *De Telegraaf*, 'Wilders over asielmaatregelen: "De PVV wacht niet langer meer!"', YouTube, 26 May 2025; https://www.pvv.nl/nieuws/geert-wilders/11561-ik-zal-niet-rusten-voor-alle-azcs-verdwenen-zijn.html.
44. F. van Benten, 'Geert Wilders zegt dat er gemiddeld iedere 11 dagen een azc bijkomt: dat klopt, maar is niet het hele verhaal', *EenVandaag*, 28 May 2025. And: 'Kunnen strengere maatregelen voor vluchtelingen verschil maken in migratiesaldo? "Asiel is een relatief klein aandeel"', *EenVandaag*, 19 May 2025.
45. 'Kabinet wankelt na overleg over asielplannen Wilders', YouTube, 3 June 2025.
46. T. Lash, 'Weer wint Wilders: het abnormale wordt normaal', *De Correspondent*, 4 June 2025.
47. 'Samenvatting adviezen Asielnoodmaatregelenwet en Wet invoering tweestatusstelsel', Council of State, 10 February 2025.
48. AFP-Agence France Presse, 'White House Backs Dutch Far-Right Leader After Government Falls', Barrons, 4 June 2025, https://

www.barrons.com/news/white-house-backs-dutch-far-right-leader-after-government-falls-61953e2d.

49. For example, in X posts by Tom Van Grieken from Vlaams Belang (3 June 2025) and Marine Le Pen (9 June 2025).

50. The so-called baseline for protecting the constitution, fundamental rights and democratic rule of law: B. van der Braak, 'Er was eens een basislijn, toch?', parlement.com, 28 February 2025.

51. According to the Red Cross, there are between 23,000 and 58,000 undocumented people in the Netherlands: 'Ondersteuning ongedocumenteerde migranten', Rode Kruis.

52. Two months later, in a letter to the Dutch parliament (29 August 2025), outgoing minister for asylum and migration Martijn van Weel rolled back criminalizing assistance to people staying illegally in the Netherlands after the Council of State ruled that limited help, such as offering a bowl of soup, could be interpreted as complicity. He upheld the criminalization of illegal stays in the Netherlands.

53. Following a request from the Dutch Senate, still to adopt a position on the bill, the outgoing Minister of Housing and Spatial Planning, Mona Keijzer, carried out further analysis of the legal validity of the law. She concluded that the amendment proposing a total ban on priority for residence permit holders… was in conflict with Article 1 of the Dutch constitution which states that everyone in a similar situation in the Netherlands must be treated equally and that discrimination is prohibited.' 'Keijzer onderzoekt uitvoerbaarheid amendementen Wet regie', Rijksoverheid, 26 August 2025.

54. 'Zorgen in Eerste Kamer over mogelijk discriminerend onderdeel Woningwet', NOS , 8 July 2025.

55. 'Stemmingen', Debat Direct, 3 July 2025 (minute 12:42).

56. G. Wilders, 'Welke PVV-Fan Wil Met Me Mee Naar de Efteling En in de Droomvlucht? Ik Trakteer! De Tien Leukste, Indrukwekkendste En Origineelste Reacties Krijgen Een Uitnodiging! Mail Naar: Efteling@pvv.Nl https://T.Co/xs2igBw7ND', X, 4 July 2025, https://x.com/geertwilderspvv/status/1941207997889524089, accessed 27 February 2026. The trip took place on 25 August 2025: Faye van Os, 'Wilders bezoekt samen met fans Efteling, maar gaat maar in één attractie', *Brabants Dagblad*, 25 August 2025.

57. https://open.spotify.com/episode/1HbGJxjOYCG1zF5ryPOsqz?si=c384e1700fb143b6&nd=1&dlsi=3ca172ef1e9c408b.

58. Nationaal Coördinator Terrorismebestrijding en Veiligheid, https://www.nctv.nl/onderwerpen/d/dtn/rechts-terrorisme-en—extremisme.

59. Kamerdebat over Geweld in Den Haag: 'Polarisatie, Verantwoordelijkheid En de Rol van de Politie', 25 September 2025, https://www.youtube.com/watch?v=SIBYy1ViOxA, BNR YouTube.

60. G. Bakker and J. Kommandeur, *HCSS Focus Complot in context*, December 2025, https://hcss.nl/wp-content/uploads/2025/12/HCSS-Focus-Complot-in-Context-HCSS-2025.pdf.

61. Z. Bogdanovic, 'Hoe de extreemrechtse omvolkingstheorie haar weg vond van de marge naar de woonkamer', Trouw, 8 October 2025, https://www.trouw.nl/binnenland/hoe-de-extreemrechtse-omvolkingstheorie-haar-weg-vond-van-de-marge-naar-de-woonkamer~b7279e0b/.

62. Bakker and Kommandeur, *HCSS Focus Complot in context*.

63. M. Rooduijn e.a., 'Liberale democratie als onderdeel van de politieke strijd', *Stuk Rood Vlees*, 22 November 2023.

64. Interview with Matthijs Rooduijn on 7 July 2025.

65. At least one in ten PVV supporters didn't even vote in the Dutch parliamentary elections in 2025; 17 per cent voted for other parties in the far-right block, such as Forum voor Democratie, JA21 and BBB; and 17 per cent shifted towards the political centre. https://nos.nl/collectie/14006/artikel/2588466-d66-snoept-stemmen-weg-van-alle-grote-partijen-ook-van-de-pvv.

66. Léonie de Jonge wrote an article on the 'cordon sanitaire' and how effective it was: 'Cordon Sanitaire', *De Groene Amsterdammer* , 5 March 2025.

67. G. Wilders, 'Geert Wilders for Breitbart: Europe May Again Need America to Liberate It', Breitbart, 12 February 2026, https://www.breitbart.com/europe/2026/02/12/europe-may-again-need-america-to-liberate-it/.

68. Interview with Federico Finchelstein on 28 December 2025.

69. 'Vertrouwen in eerlijke verkiezingen – een verkenning van de publieke opinie', Kiesraaad, https://www.kiesraad.nl/adviezen-en-publicaties/publicaties/2022/2/3/vertrouwen-in-eerlijke-verkiezingen.

70. Interview with Jelle Postma on 31 October 2025.

71. Interview with Federico Finchelstein on 28 December 2025.

72. Paxton, *The Anatomy of Fascism*.

73. Some professors in political science still classify his approach as 'far-right populism', because, says Matthijs Rooduijn: 'Wilders wants to strangle democratic rule of law, but he doesn't go as far as glorifying violence'. Sarah de Lange notes, however, that there has already been a shift on the scale from radical-right populism to extreme-right: 'In recent years, the PVV has gradually adopted

ever more extreme positions. He's in a grey area because there are definitely extreme-right elements in his proposals.' Catherine de Vries thinks that he's already gone past that point: 'His positions are definitely extreme-right'.

74. J. P. Stroobants, 'Dutch far-right leader claims world is governed by "evil reptiles"', *Le Monde*, 21 October 2022, https://www. lemonde.fr/en/international/article/2022/10/21/dutch-far-right-leader-claims-world-is-governed-by-evil-reptiles_6001236_4.html.

75. T. Baudet, 'Westen lijdt aan auto-immuunziekte', *Forum voor Democratie*, speech 15 Jan 2017, https://fvd.nl/nieuws/ toespraak-thierry-baudet-alv-fvd-2017.

76. https://www.nrc.nl/nieuws/2026/02/04/opmars-van-extreemrechts-op-kandidatenlijsten-van-fvd-a4919396.

77. Interview with Thomas Weber on 30 March 2026.

5. Together against fascism

1.   Klein and Taylor, 'The Rise of End Times Fascism'.
2.   E. Temelkuran, 'Can the Term "Cloud Fascism" Help Us Understand – and Resist – the Hard Right?'
3.   T. Snyder, *On Tyranny: Twenty Lessons from the Twentieth Century*, Penguin Random House, 2017.
4.   Amazon deleted all references to diversity and inclusion from its annual report: A. Palmer, 'Amazon Scrubs DEI Mention from Its Annual Report', CNBC, 7 February 2025, https://www. cnbc.com/2025/02/07/amazon-scrubs-dei-mention-from-its-annual-report.html. Deloitte reportedly asked staff to delete their pronouns from e-mail signatures and has stopped drafting reports on diversity and inclusion: E. Kissin and M. McCormick, 'Deloitte Asks Consultants to US Government to Remove Gender Pronouns from Emails', *Financial Times*, 11 February 2025, https://www.ft.com/content/1230c47d-6b93-4b8d-8f2a-175b7e01c31e Dutch companies are also changing their approach: ASML and Philips are applying an amended policy in the US that does not include specific diversity and inclusion targets, yet they continue to do so in other countries: Eumedion, *Evaluation of the 2025 AGM Season*, Eumedion, 9 July 2025, https://www.eumedion.nl/clientdata/215/media/clientimages/ Evaluation-AGM-season-2025-DEF.pdf. Ageon scrapped its target for more women in top positions, and Arcadis replaced a bonus for achieving gender diversity targets with a bonus for a different target: Wilco Dekker, 'Nederlandse bedrijven passen

diversiteitsdoelen aan vanwege Trump, die inclusief beleid verbiedt', *De Volkskrant*, 9 July 2025.

5.   'Steeds minder scholen doen mee aan Week van de Lentekriebels: "Moeten leraren vertrouwen"', WNL, 31 March 2025.

6.   M. Savage, 'BBC Tells Staff They Cannot Quote Trump Line Removed from Reith Lecture', *The Guardian*, 27 November 2025, https://www.theguardian.com/media/2025/nov/27/bbc-donald-trump-corruption-line-removed-from-rutger-bregman-reith-lecture.

7.   Menno Hurenkamp, 'Waarom is Nederland zo verrechtst? Drie schrijvers zoeken naar een antwoord', *NRC*, 6 June 2025.

8.   Sjoerd de Jong, 'Jacht op "ideologische stuff" in wetenschap is in VS geopend', *NRC*, 26 March 2025.

9.   Folkert van der Krol, 'Artiesten Big Rivers mogen zich niet politiek uiten: "Geschrokken van wat er rond Douwe Bob gebeurde"', *AD*, 12 July 2025.

10. R. Ben-Ghiat, 'Resistance Tips', *Lucid*, 14 June 2025, https://lucid.substack.com/p/resistance-tips.

11. On 1 August 2025, the mayor of Budapest, Gergely Karácsony, was questioned by the police as a suspect who helped the city's Pride organizers. The Hungarian National Bureau of Investigation, which is tasked with investigating serious and complex crimes, said it had launched a probe against an 'unknown perpetrator' accused of organizing the rally.

12. Snyder, *On Tyranny*, p. 115.

13. Rinke Verkerk, 'De journalistiek faalt, ziet deze journalist op de Westelijke Jordaanoever. "De werkelijkheid is te pijnlijk. Ze geloven het simpelweg niet"', *De Correspondent*, 16 July 2025.

14. Erica Chenoweth, *Questions, Answers, and Some Cautionary Updates Regarding the 3.5% Rule*, Carr Center Discussion Paper 2020-005, Harvard Kennedy School, Spring 2020, https://www.hks.harvard.edu/sites/default/files/2024-05/Erica%20Chenoweth_2020-005.pdf.

6. The foundations: politics that fight back

1.   Like Catherine de Vries, a professor of political science and President of the Institute for European Policymaking at the Bocconi University, Milan, and Matthijs Rooduijn, a political scientist at the University of Amsterdam, to whom I spoke on 7 July 2025.

2.   T. Orbán, *Patriots Take EU Parliament to Court Over Undemocratic Cordon Sanitaire*, *The European Conservative* 1 October 2024,

https://europeanconservative.com/articles/news/patriots-take-eu-parliament-to-court-over-undemocratic-cordon-sanitaire/.

3.   'SPD beschließt Vorbereitung von AfD-Verbotsverfahren', *Die Zeit*, 29 June 2025.

4.   'Wet op de politieke partijen', parlement.com, accessed on 18 September 2025.

5.   'Braziliaanse rechters sluiten Bolsonaro uit van verkiezingen tot 2030', 30 June 2023, NOS, https://nos.nl/artikel/2480958-braziliaanse-rechters-sluiten-bolsonaro-uit-van-verkiezingen-tot-2030?.

6.   K. Armstrong, 'Brazil: Bolsonaro Ordered to Start Serving 27-Year Prison Sentence for Coup Plot', BBC, 26 November 2025, https://www.bbc.com/news/articles/cr4dl19npv5o.

7.   Snyder, *On Tyranny*.

8.   M. Bray, *Antifa: The Anti-Fascist Handbook*, Melville House Publishing, 2017.

9.   Bert van der Braak, 'De waarde van eed of belofte', parlement.com, 15 August 2025.

10. Marton Dunai, 'Hungarian opposition groups quit to make way for Orbán challenger', *Financial Times*, 26 February 2026, https://www.ft.com/content/85210187-c757-4432-bb57-6b636a669e72?syn-25a6b1a6=1.

11. R. Tait, 'Hungary Opposition Figures Urge Democrats to Organize against Autocratic Takeover by Trump', *The Guardian*, 16 July 2025, https://www.theguardian.com/us-news/2025/jul/16/hungary-democrat-authoritarianism.

12. A. Marquez, 'Zohran Mamdani Says He Still Believes Trump Is a "Fascist" and a "Despot" after White House Meeting', NBC News, 23 November 2025, https://www.nbcnews.com/politics/donald-trump/zohran-mamdani-trump-fascist-despot-white-house-meeting-rcna245309.

13. Zohran Mamdani, 'Know Your Rights When Dealing With ICE', YouTube, 7 December 2025, https://www.youtube.com/watch?v=Tq-KqQXy4LE.

14. R. Tait, 'Hungary Opposition Figures Urge Democrats to Organize against Autocratic Takeover by Trump', *The Guardian*, 16 July 2025, https://www.theguardian.com/us-news/2025/jul/16/hungary-democrat-authoritarianism.

15. K. Laycock, 'Inside Europe 12 June 2025' Dw.Com, 12 June 2025, https://www.dw.com/en/inside-europe-12-june-2025/audio-72891488.

16. G. Wilders, 'Einde Oefening NSC. #DEBAT #PVV #StemPVV https://T.Co/DQH3thJmE0', X, 27 August 2025, https://x.com/geertwilderspvv/status/1960676630008934881.

17. 'Fighting the Oligarchy': AOC, Bernie Blast Trump "Corruption"
    Urge Dems to Fight Harder', MSNBC YouTube, 20 March 2025,
    https://www.youtube.com/watch?v=wADb1lfxRZM.
18. P. Magyar on Facebook, 10 February 2024, https://
    www.facebook.com/photo?fbid=7670871072947274&se
    t=a.115525025148621.
19. R. Ben-Ghiat, 'Hope: The Secret Weapon of Democracy
    Protection', *Lucid*, 24 May 2022, https://lucid.substack.com/p/
    hope-the-secret-weapon-of-democracy.
20. R. Ben-Ghiat, 'Why Joy Is an Effective Anti-Authoritarian
    Strategy.' *Lucid*, 29 August 2024, https://lucid.substack.com/p/
    why-joy-is-an-effective-anti-authoritarian.
21. J. Cienski, 'Huge but Glum: Poland's Opposition
    Puts a Million People on the Streets', *Politico*, 1
    October 2023, https://www.politico.eu/article/
    poland-tusk-million-hearts-civic-coalition-warsaw.
22. E. Klein, 'Mamdani, Trump and the End of the Old Politics',
    The New York Times, 28 June 2025, https://www.nytimes.
    com/2025/06/28/opinion/ezra-klein-show-chris-hayes.html.
23. 'Rob Jetten', *Politico*, 9 December 2025, https://www.politico.eu/
    list/politico-28-class-of-2026/rob-jetten/.
24. 'NSC stemt in met asielwetten, met ruimte voor
    medemenselijkheid', *NSC*, 3 July 2025.
25. 'Inside Europe 12 June 2025', Dw.com, 12 June 2025, https://
    www.dw.com/en/inside-europe-12-june-2025/audio-72891488.
26. K. Goethals and C. van de Ven, '"Ik wandel door een mijnenveld"',
    De Groene Amsterdammer, 5 June 2024.

7. The protective layer: resilient journalism

1. M. Lewis, 'Has Anyone Seen the President?', Bloomberg,
    9 February 2018, https://www.bloomberg.com/view/
    articles/2018-02-09/has-anyone-seen-the-president.
2. J. Rosen, 'Leugens van politici tegenspreken is geen
    vooringenomenheid. Het is de plicht van elke journalist', *De
    Correspondent*, 29 September 2020, https://decorrespondent.
    nl/11649/leugens-van-politici-tegenspreken-is-geen-
    vooringenomenheid-het-is-de-plicht-van-elke-journalist/.
3. Bolet and F. Foos, 'Media Platforming and the Normalisation of
    Extreme Right Views', *British Journal of Political Science*, 55, 2025,
    e103, https://doi.org/10.1017/S0007123425000195.
4. 'Hegseth Accuses Journalist of 'Peddling Hoaxes' after Secret

Yemen War Plans Shared on App', *The Guardian*, YouTube, 25 March 2025, https://www.youtube.com/watch?v=iEfBbXEVVRg.

5. Jay Rosen, 'Four Radical Ways the Media Can Protect US Democracy from Trump', *The Correspondent*, 21 October 2020, https://thecorrespondent.com/757/four-radical-ways-the-media-can-protect-us-democracy-from-trump.

6. A. Kouwenhoven and L. Levy, 'Een zelfbenoemde "burgerwacht" organiseerde grenscontroles: "Helaas troffen we geen asielzoekers aan"', *NRC*, 10 juni 2025.

7. For an excellent example of this, see: R. Verkerk, 'Israël gijzelt duizenden Palestijnen in martelkampen. Amin overleefde dat zeven keer', *De Correspondent*, 17 April 2025.

8. The New Arab Staff, 'NYT Op-Ed Finally Breaks Western Media Silence on Gaza Genocide', *The New Arab*, 16 July 2025, https://www.newarab.com/news/nyt-op-ed-finally-breaks-western-media-silence-gaza-genocide.

9. L. Aharouay et al., 'Trump, zegt premier Dick Schoof, kan een "beslissende" rol spelen in de wereldvrede', *NRC*, 25 June 2025, https://www.nrc.nl/nieuws/2025/06/25/trump-zegt-premier-dick-schoof-kan-een-beslissende-rol-spelen-in-de-wereldvrede-a4898352.

10. J. Rosen, 'Autocraten zaaien chaos en verwarring. Dit is wat journalisten ertegen kunnen doen', *De Correspondent*, 7 October 2020, https://decorrespondent.nl/11686/autocraten-zaaien-chaos-en-verwarring-dit-is-wat-journalisten-ertegen-kunnen-doen/eb5f8ece-3441-04e7-0bbe-c7b5787c5c1d.

11. Like they did with the Panama Papers, for example: M. T. Ronderos and A. Lipstas, 'The Investigative Journalism Collaboration That Produced the Panama Papers', Voices – Open Society Foundations, 8 April 2016, https://www.opensocietyfoundations.org/voices/investigative-journalism-collaboration-produced-panama-papers.

12. According to this recent UK study, nine out of ten journalists come from a white background: I. Henkel, 'The Personal Characteristics and Diversity of UK Journalists', Reuters Institute for the Study of Journalism, 23 April 2025, http://reutersinstitute.politics.ox.ac.uk/uk-journalists-2020s/1-personal-characteristics-and-diversity-uk-journalists.

13. As happened to the Italian-Palestinian journalist Rula Jabreal, for example: 'Italy: Rula Jebreal Faces Lawsuit for Criticizing Government', Coalition For Women in Journalism, 19 January 2024, https://www.womeninjournalism.org/infocus-all/transnational-repression; and the British journalist Carole

Cadwalladr: 'This Is What a Digital Coup Looks Like', TED, YouTube, 10 April 2025, https://www.youtube.com/watch?v=TZOoT8AbkNE.

8. The barrier: society in solidarity

1. E. K. Ward, 'The Other Big Lie', Western States Center, Medium, 12 January 2022, https://westernstatescenter.medium.com/the-other-big-lie-c3d6d7c9f31.
2. H. Arendt, *The Origins of Totalitarianism*, London, Penguin Classics, 2017. First published in 1951.
3. H. Arendt, *The Life of the Mind*, New York, Harcourt Brace Jovanovich, 1977.
4. E. Nehorai, 'It's Time to Start Thinking About Your Safety', Elad Nehorai's Substack newsletter, 17 July 2024, https://eladnehorai.substack.com/p/its-time-to-start-thinking-about.
5. D. Gate, *A Rebellion of Care: Poems and Essays*, New York, Convergent Books, 2023.
6. Read more here: 'Civil Servants and the Constitution | LinkedIn', https://www.linkedin.com/company/ambtenaren-en-de-grondwet-90, accessed 20 January 2026.
7. D. Gate, 'Why Kindness Alone Is Not Enough', *A Rebellion of Care*, Substack newsletter, 2 August 2025, https://davidgate.substack.com/p/why-kindness-alone-is-not-enough.
8. M. L. King, *Stride Toward Freedom: The Montgomery Story*, New York, Harper & Row Publishers, 1958.
9. T. Snyder, '20 Lessons from the 20th Century', Tr@nsit Online, n.d., https://www.iwm.at/transit-online/20-lessons-from-the-20th-century.
10. Z. Kanno-Youngs et al., 'Trump Invokes Kirk's Killing in Justifying Measures to Silence Opponents', *The New York Times*, 17 September 2025, https://www.nytimes.com/2025/09/16/us/politics/trump-kirk-free-speech-hate-speech-left.html.
11. P. Achard et al., 'Local exposure to refugees changed attitudes to ethnic minorities in the Netherlands', *The Economic Journal*, vol.135, no. 667, April 2025, p. 808–837, https://doi.org/10.1093/ej/ueae080.
12. Learn more at the Deep Canvas Institute: https://www.deepcanvass.org/.
13. D. Broockman and J. Kalla, 'Durably Reducing Transphobia: A Field Experiment on Door-to-Door Canvassing', *Science*, vol. 352, no. 6282, 2016, p. 220–4, https://doi.org/10.1126/science.aad9713.

14. K. Chatterjee, 'On Getting Unf*cked', *Pulling Ourselves Together*, Substack newsletter, 22 February 2025, https://pullingtogether. substack.com/p/on-getting-unfcked.

15. R. Ben-Ghiat, 'Why Joy Is an Effective Anti-Authoritarian Strategy', *Lucid*, Substack newsletter, 29 August 2024, https://lucid.substack. com/p/why-joy-is-an-effective-anti-authoritarian.

16. A. Fields-Meyer, 'Find a Political Home', *You Are Here by Ami Fields-Meyer*, Substack newsletter, 11 November 2024, https:// amifieldsmeyer.substack.com/p/find-a-political-home.

17. H. Siddique, 'Massive Attack Announce Alliance of Musicians Speaking out over Gaza', *The Guardian*, 17 July 2025, https://www. theguardian.com/music/2025/jul/17/massive-attack-announce-alliance-of-musicians-speaking-out-over-gaza.

18. For the Dutch figures, see: https://www.electionguide. org/countries/id/152/. For the UK, see the Electoral Commissions 2024 and 2025 reports: https://www. electoralcommission.org.uk/research-reports-and-data/ our-reports-and-data-past-elections-and-referendums.

19. 'The 2020 and 2024 presidential contests were among the highest-turnout elections in the past century. The 66% turnout rate in 2020 was the highest since 1908, and 2024's rate of 64% was the second highest, tied with 1960.' https://www.pewresearch.org/ politics/2025/06/26/voter-turnout-2020-2024/.

20. The average voter turnout in national elections in European countries is 66.5 per cent. Our World in Data, 'Voter turnout of registered voters' https://ourworldindata.org/grapher/voter-turnout-of-registered-voters (accessed on 17 March 2026).

21. https://results.elections.europa.eu/en/turnout/ (accessed on 17 March 2026).